SHOOTING.

With
GAME & GUN ROOM NOTES.

by
"Blagdon."

Read Country Books
Home Farm
44 Evesham Road
Cookhill, Alcester
Warwickshire
B49 5LJ

www.readcountrybooks.com

© Read Books 2005
This book is copyright and may not be
reproduced or copied in any way without
the express permission of the publisher in writing.

ISBN No. 1-905124-69-4

Published by Read Country Books 2005

British Library Cataloguing-in-Publication Data
A catalogue record for this book is available
from the British Library.

Read Country Books
Home Farm
44 Evesham Road
Cookhill, Alcester
Warwickshire
B49 5LJ

SHOOTING.

WITH

GAME AND GUN-ROOM NOTES.

By " Blagdon."

A Comprehensive Book of HOW TO SHOOT.

GUN FITTING. GROUSE.
MODERN GUNS. PARTRIDGE.
AMMUNITION. PHEASANT.
LIVE & INANIMATE BIRD SHOOTING.

Very Extensively Illustrated with Full-Page and Other-sized Drawings
and Photographs from Life.

The Drawings by Archibald Thorburn, Henry Stannard, and Others.

———

London:

COGSWELL AND HARRISON, Limited.

1900

(All Rights Reserved.)

SCHULTZE GUNPOWDER

TRADE  MARK.

Highest Honours wherever Exhibited.

LONDON	...	1885	CALIFORNIA	...	1894	MILAN	...	1894
CHICAGO	...	1893	ANTWERP	...	1894	ATLANTA	...	1895
		BRUSSELS	...	...	...	1897.		

"SCHULTZE" THE ORIGINAL SMOKELESS POWDER.

PIGEON SHOOTING.

All Principal Events at Home and Abroad have been won with SCHULTZE POWDER.

The Amateur Championship of America	...	...	...	...	1895
The Professional Championship of America	...	...	...	...	1895
The Championship at Spa	...	...	...	...	...	1895
The Championship at Aix-les-Bains	...	...	...	...	1895
The Championship at Bosnia	...	...	...	...	1896
The Champion Stakes (Hurlingham)	...	...	...	...	1896
The Champion Stakes (Gun Club) Divided	...	...	...	1896
The Amateur Championship of America	...	...	...	1897
The Challenge Cup, Melbourne	...	...	...	...	1897
The Gun Club Challenge Cup won outright	...	...	...	1897
The Triennial Championship (Monte Carlo)	...	...	...1889 to 1898
The Grand Prix du Casino (Monte Carlo)	...	...	...	1898
The Grand Prix du Cloture (Monte Carlo)	...	...	...	1898
The Grand American Handicap, 197 Competitors	...	...	1898
The Gun Club £100 Challenge Cup won outright	...	...	1898
The Belgium £100 Cup (International Meeting)	...	...	1898
The Gun Club £200 International Cup	...	...	...	1898
The Grande Poule D'Essai (Monte Carlo), 103 Competitors	...	1899
The Prix D'Ouverture (Monte Carlo), 117 Competitors	...	...	1899
The Gun Club International Cup	...	...	...	...	1900
The Members' Challenge Cup (International Meeting)	...	...	1900
The 32 yards Sweepstakes	...	...	...	...	...	1900

SUPPLIED IN CANISTERS AND CARTRIDGES.

—WHOLESALE ONLY—

THE SCHULTZE GUNPOWDER Co., Ltd.
28, GRESHAM STREET, LONDON, E.C.

INTRODUCTION.

In writing this book, it is the desire to place before the Shooting World a work of concise form.

The notes and suggestions on Guns, Ammunition, and Game Shooting may possibly be of some interest to the devotee of that sport, but more particularly of service to that ever numerous body—the less experienced.

It is not contended that the whole of the matters treated on are original, but the endeavour has been to put the various subjects in a sufficiently brief but yet concise form.

The specimens given of Guns, Shooting School, etc., and such like are simply quoted as examples of the very best type of to-day.

The photographs generally included in "How to Shoot" and elsewhere are from life, being taken at the Blagdon Shooting School.

The well-executed drawings by Archibald Thorburn, Henry Stannard, and others are from the "Badminton Magazine" and Hudson's "British Birds."

That these papers will produce some interest, and possibly good effect, is the wish of the writer, who adopts the nom de plume of

"BLAGDON."

July, 1900.

CONTENTS.

HOW TO SHOOT.

To shoot well—The kind of gun—How to take the bird—
How far in front—Finding the point—Allowance—
Swing—Which is the easiest shot?—Practice necessary—The straight-away shot—Going away, with side
inclination—The skimming shot—Right and left shots—
Driven birds—Driven Partridges—Practice makes perfect—Woodcock—Snipe . . .. **1—21**

GUN-FITTING.

Science of gun-fitting—Specialists—Faults may be remedied—Shooting schools—The shooting is seen to improve—The gun of correct shape—Alignment controlled
by the eye—The master eye—The left eye the stronger **22—30**

MODERN GUNS.

Hammerless gun — Ejector gun — Single-trigger gun —
The cost of a gun—The superiority of a best gun—
Bores and weights—Gun barrels—Barrel tube manu-
facture — A good shooting gun — Shot-gun patterns —
The game gun — The long-range gun — Ball and shot
guns—Various bores—Penetration—The proof of guns—
Nitro proof—Undue risks : Dangerous experiments—
To prolong the life of the gun—Cleaning—Annual in-
spection... ... ... **31—43**

AMMUNITION.

Smokeless powder—Cartridge cases—Cap testing—Wads—
Shot—Powder pressures—Crusher gauge—Penetration—
Velocities—Patterns—Recoil—A standardised cartridge—
Hang-fires—Gun strikers—Shot velocities for given dis-
tances—Remaining shot velocities—Energy—Rates of
flight of birds... ... ... **44—58**

CONTENTS.

GROUSE SHOOTING.

PAGE

Popularity of grouse shooting—Going grouse shooting—Arrival at the moor—Scotch and English moors—Driving—The best performers ... ... 59—77

PARTRIDGE SHOOTING.

The partridge and the plough—Water—Rights of way—The farmer of the land—Vermin—A good keeper—Shots out of range—Walking-up—Driving—Considerable practice—Many invitations ... ... 78—91

PHEASANT SHOOTING.

Laying in captivity—Cost of pheasant rearing—The head of game—Movable pens—In hunting localities—The old style of shooting—A fine October day ... ... 92—102

PIGEON SHOOTING.

Penetration—Pattern—Good balance—Hurlingham Club rules—Gun Club rules—General pigeon shooting rules—Boundary ... ... 103—113

INANIMATE BIRD SHOOTING.

What is the bird?—Effect of inanimate bird shooting—Official rules—The "Rose" system of dividing ... ... 114—121

Legal seasons for killing game, etc. 122

LIST OF ILLUSTRATIONS.

	PAGE
"The man who didn't"	1
Walking up: Dangerous—safe	2
Carrying a gun: Safe—dangerous—safe	3
Loading pair of guns: No. 1 position—No. 2 position	4
Straight-away rising shot...	8
Going away, rising and crossing...	9
Straight-away skimming shot	10
Skimming right to left shot	11
Crossing right to left up sloping bank	12
Vertical shot—holding well back	13
Crossing left to right down sloping bank	14
Approaching high shot	15
Overhead shot on the right	16
Brace of birds: Right barrel coming—Left barrel going	17
"Mark 'cock!" (by Henry Stannard)	19
Gun-fitting (examples)	22
Try-gun	23
Gun-fitting: Right and left shots	25
Gun-fitting: Elevation	26
Gun-fitting: Rising bird	27
Gun-fitting: Alignment	29
Cross-eyed gun	30
Lever over guard gun	31
Top-lever gun	31
Hammerless gun	32

LIST OF ILLUSTRATIONS.

vii

	PAGE
Details of patent ejector	33
Details of single-trigger gun	34
Modern gun	35
Steel and Damascus barrels	36
Gun-barrel boring	37
Ball and shot gun	39
Shooting at fifty yards of ball and shot gun : 10-bore ...	40
Cap tester	45
Crusher gauge	48
"When the blissful Twelfth came round " (by Henry Stannard) ...	61
"You never know what will get up " (by Henry Stannard)... ...	65
"Bring them down neatly and well " (by Henry Stannard) ...	69
"Upwards and over the guns " (by Archibald Thorburn)	73
"The little brown bird " (by G. E. Lodge)	78
"Early Morning " (by Henry Stannard)	81
"Their number reduced by one " (by Henry Stannard) ...	87
"Back come some birds " (by N. Arthur Loraine)	90
"Through the bracken " (by Archibald Thorburn)	93
"Rocketting Pheasants " (by Archibald Thorburn)	97
"The rearing of your birds " (by N. Arthur Loraine)	100
"Grand Prix " pigeon gun	103
The blue rock pigeon—male and female	105
Improved model "Swiftsure "	121

LONDON:
PRINTED BY THE BURLINGTON PUBLISHING CO., LTD.,
72, 73, 74, 75, & 76 TEMPLE CHAMBERS, E.C.

SHOOTING.

HOW TO SHOOT

THE remarks in this chapter are not intended for those who are past-masters in the art of shooting. They are meant rather for those who are, from one cause or another, dissatisfied with their shooting, and for the novice, who has everything to learn; at the same time, it is hoped that there may be found amongst them something that will be of interest to shooting men in general.

THE MAN WHO DIDN'T.

TO SHOOT WELL.

To shoot well—at any rate, to become an average shot—is the ambition of every man who takes any interest in shooting. In this, as in all other sports and pastimes, there is a vast difference between some men and others. There are men, though they are few and far between,

Dangerous.   **WALKING UP.**   Safe.

who, like some cricketers who are born batsmen, seem to find no difficulty from the very first in handling and using a gun to good effect, while there are others who might, unaided, spend half a lifetime in trying to acquire the art, without much success. It is not necessary to say much about the former class, except that they seem able to shoot to a certain extent with almost any gun, because they are naturally quick at discovering, after firing a few shots with any particular gun,

HOW TO SHOOT.

any peculiarities which that gun may happen to have, and they are able, after a little practice, to put the gun to the shoulder in such a manner as to bring it "dead on" the object often enough to make what is considered to be good shooting. But, as regards the latter class of shooters, such men are to be met with every day. It is for these that that great triumph of the modern gunmaker's art—the adjustable

Safe.   Dangerous.   Safe.
CARRYING A GUN.

try-gun—was invented, and by its use much time and money, which otherwise might have been wasted in useless practice, are saved. The reason of this is obvious. It has already been remarked that the man who is naturally an adept with the shot-gun is quick to detect any fault in himself or his gun, and is able, to a greater or less degree, to rectify the error, so as to make a fair proportion of hits to misses, and

4   SHOOTING.

it is this very quality that is lacking in the other men; therefore, something must be done to supply the deficiency.

THE KIND OF GUN.

No further allusion need be made here to the try-gun, as this is not intended to be a treatise on gun-fitting, but there can be no

No. 1 Position.   No. 2 Position.
LOADING PAIR OF GUNS.

harm in reminding the reader that the try-gun, in the hands of an inexperienced instructor, is a weapon worse than useless to one who, by its aid, hopes to obtain a gun that fits him, and thereby improve his shooting. Nor need any apology be made for referring to the necessity of every man who would shoot his best having a perfectly-fitting gun, for it is obviously impossible for anyone to

HOW TO SHOOT.

become such a good workman as he would be if only provided with bad or indifferent tools. Nor, on the other hand, will he, because he is the fortunate possessor of a weapon perfect in every detail, both as regards fit and manufacture, necessarily become a good shot without further trouble.

HOW TO TAKE THE BIRD.

There are other points to which he must pay the closest attention. Of these, perhaps, the most important is the acquirement of the knowledge how to "take" the different shots that offer themselves—that is to say, he must, knowing that he has in his hands a reliable weapon, try to note with exactness the position of the bird with reference to the muzzle of his gun, when properly aligned at the moment of pressing the trigger. He will then, in the case of a miss, and assuming that his ammunition is, as it should be, of the best, know that he has made a miscalculation of some sort; it may be either of time, angle, distance, or rate of speed at which the object aimed at was moving.

HOW FAR IN FRONT.

Many a man who is a first-rate shot has been asked to explain how it is that he is able to kill with such frequency; and what a difficult question it is to answer! The commonest form in which the query is put is the following: "How far did you shoot in front of that fast crossing bird you just killed?" (The bird, maybe, was going at the rate of thirty to forty miles an hour.) Then it is that the shooter is nonplussed. He really does not know; and how should he? What man can estimate with exactness the distance that he aimed in front of a fast crossing bird, especially when it is remembered that his calculations had to be made in a something many times less than a second? Occasionally, however, someone will hazard a conjecture, and in reply to the above query make answer that to the best of his belief he held ten feet in front of the bird. Another man asked the same question will say twenty feet, perhaps, and yet each of these men, and under exactly similar

6 SHOOTING.

conditions, are able to kill their bird time after time in spite of the fact that their ideas as to how far ahead they shoot differ so widely. The fact of the matter is that both these men shoot at a spot in front of the bird which experience has proved for them· selves to be the correct one, and there is nothing to prove that the estimate of either of them as to the actual distance in feet at the moment of firing between the " spot " they aimed at and the bird itself is a correct one.

Then there is the man who says he puts up his gun and shoots straight at the bird or " holds " on to its beak—for everyone makes some sort of attempt at getting forward—and yet he, too, shoots as successfully, perhaps, as those who maintain that they shoot many feet in front. But it is not so much a matter of importance as to how far one aims in front of a bird as to what one does during the time that elapses between " finding the point" in front of the bird and the moment at which the trigger is pulled. This is the part of the question most frequently overlooked, and it is because of this that many a man who believed he was well in front of his bird has missed it altogether.

FINDING THE POINT.

After one has " found the point," or, in other words, made up one's mind, the aim being considered satisfactory, to pull the trigger, a certain amount of time, infinitesimal though it may be, does elapse before the trigger is actually pulled; the hammer then falls, the striker is driven home, and the cartridge is fired in a space of time so short that these different actions may be almost said to be simultaneous—but all this time, short though it may be, the bird is moving. And, after the cartridge is fired, the shot will take a fraction of a second to reach the bird, and in that fraction of a second the object aimed at will travel a certain distance.

ALLOWANCE.

It is possible that the reason why some men make a greater allowance in front of a bird than others is the fact of their being slower, after making up their minds to fire, in pulling the trigger. It is very

HOW TO SHOOT.

evident that, if a man, even though the muzzle of his gun may point many feet in the front of a bird at the moment that he makes up his mind to fire, is slow in pulling the trigger, or fails to "swing" both before and after so doing, the chances are that he will be behind, or only just touch the bird with the outside pellets of the charge.

" SWING."

It is this "swing" as the trigger is pressed that imparts to the shot as it leaves the barrel a forward motion, rendered necessary to compensate for the time that the charge takes in reaching the object. Often and often one meets with a man who swings his gun well up in front of a bird, and then, at the moment of firing, suddenly arrests the movement, bringing his gun to a full stop altogether, with the natural result that the shot passes behind the bird. It must not be supposed, however, that in using the term "swing" it is meant that one should follow a bird on for a considerable distance before pulling the trigger. Such a style of shooting is very often dangerous to other persons, not to mention the fact that the bird is often out of range before the shot is fired.

WHICH IS THE EASIEST SHOT?

It is a moot point as to which, if we except the straight going-away and horizontal shot, is the easiest of all other chances that one gets in the shooting field. Some men prefer the crossing shot at right angles, either to the left or right, while others maintain that a bird coming straight to you, that you shoot at at an angle, before it gets to you, is the least difficult. The whole question depends probably more on the amount of practice that one gets at each kind of shot than on anything else.

PRACTICE NECESSARY.

A man must have practice of some sort, and this can best be obtained by the use of inanimate birds thrown from a trap, by which means an unlimited amount of shooting can be indulged in at birds going at every conceivable angle and in every possible direction.

THE STRAIGHT-AWAY SHOT.

First of all, the straight-away and rising shot may be tried, the chief thing to remember here being to keep well " on top " of the bird.

STRAIGHT-AWAY RISING SHOT.

GOING AWAY, WITH SIDE INCLINATION.

Then some birds going away, but inclining more or less to the right or left, should be taken, and here it must be recollected that the bird is not only going away and rising, but also crossing, from right to left or left to right, as the case may be, at an angle. The gun must, therefore, be swung up over and in front of the bird in one motion. These rapidly rising shots will be more often encountered when walking up pheasants in covert, on which occasions one sees, from lack of the above precautions, birds too frequently shot in the tail. To

HOW TO SHOOT. 9

kill a bird in the latter fashion is an error to be avoided, added to which the bird is thereby quite spoilt for the table, if, as is often the case, the shooting is at close quarters.

GOING AWAY—RISING AND CROSSING.

THE SKIMMING SHOT.

The trap may now be set a trifle lower, so that the birds skim over the ground, either straight away from or to the left or right of the shooter. These birds will be rising only gradually, so that the gun will not have to be elevated to such a degree as in the former instance. Such shots as these represent partridges as nearly as possible when walked up early in the season. If a piece of sloping ground is available, some very useful practice may be had at birds thrown

10   SHOOTING.

either up or down hill—a very useful imitation of partridges when walked up on a sloping field or of pheasants in covert on the side of a valley being by this means arrived at.

RIGHT AND LEFT SHOTS.

The shooter may now take a few shots standing away from the

STRAIGHT-AWAY SKIMMING SHOT.

trap, so that the birds cross him more or less at right angles to the line of fire—either rising or falling—the gun being brought well forward and raised or lowered according to whether the bird is getting higher or lower in its flight.

The gun-stock of every sportsman should fit to a nicety, should he wish to shoot at his best.

HOW TO SHOOT. 11

DRIVEN BIRDS.

After this, attention may be directed to practice at driven birds —high overhead—thrown from the trap fixed on to a platform or the flat roof of some building fifty feet or more from the ground. These will give a very good idea of the driven pheasant, and a great variety of shots, and some very difficult ones, will be obtained,

SKIMMING RIGHT TO LEFT SHOT.

especially if it is possible to throw the birds over trees between the platform and the shooter. First of all there is the straight over-head bird, coming at the shooter, and either rising or falling, which is perhaps the easiest of all shots at high birds. Here we have simply to remember to get the gun well up to the bird and swing well forward. The shooter should begin by standing at some distance from the trap and gradually working closer in, when he will get some very fast shots indeed, and he will have to be very quick to break his bird before it has passed over his head. After this the trap should be set so as to throw the birds to the right or left of the shooter, and he will find that some of them take a good deal of stopping. Special attention will be necessary here to take in at a glance whether the birds are rising, flying parallel with

CROSSING RIGHT TO LEFT UP SLOPING BANK.

the ground, or falling. Many men seem to have a tendency to shoot over birds of this description. There is something deceptive in the appearance of the angle to the line of fire at which the bird is going, which probably accounts for this. It is, at all times, a difficult shot, and one that requires more practice, possibly, than any.

To shoot well, use a good-fitting gun.

HOW TO SHOOT. 13

VERTICAL SHOT—HOLDING WELL BACK.

The going-away shot, high or low, at a bird that has risen from the ground in front of the shooter has already been discussed, but there still remains the overhead shot at a bird that has passed over the shooter's head—a very common one when partridge or pheasant driving, and one very often missed. It is no very easy matter, after firing the right barrel at a bird coming to one, and having missed him, to turn quickly round and kill him with the other barrel. The place to shoot is generally well underneath him, as such a bird is seldom rising, unless there is high ground or tall coppice rising suddenly, causing the bird to alter the height of its line of flight after passing the shooter.

DRIVEN PARTRIDGES.

The flight of driven partidges can be as well represented by birds thrown from the trap as can that of pheasants, but in this case the platform on which the trap is fixed should not be more than fifteen or twenty feet from the ground. It is desirable, too, that the birds should be thrown over a screen of some sort, or, better still, a heap, which will not only hide the trap from the

CROSSING LEFT TO RIGHT DOWN SLOPING BANK.

shooter but will also enable him to take his birds in the same manner and under the same conditions as he would in the field. Here, too, the shooter should begin some distance from the trap, and gradually work nearer, and he should, after attaining a fair measure of success with single birds, try some rights and lefts, if he has a double or two single traps at his disposal. The same remarks which have been made concerning the killing of driven pheasants will apply here, the only difference being that the birds are somewhat lower, and it is more easy therefore to take in at a glance the exact angle and direction of the flight of the bird.

APPROACHING HIGH SHOT.

PRACTICE MAKES PERFECT.

It is to be hoped that, after reading the foregoing remarks, the critical reader will not consider that too much space has been devoted to the question of the shooting of inanimate birds. That this style of shooting is artificial none will deny; but herein lies

OVERHEAD SHOT ON THE RIGHT.

its great advantage, for it would be obviously impossible to have live birds repeatedly flying in exactly the same fashion so as to afford continual practice to the man being coached towards the

Right Barrel Coming.   **BRACE OF BIRDS.**   Left Barrel Going.

goal of proficiency; but with inanimate birds this and more can be done, for not only can they be thrown over and over again in the same direction, but their speed can also be regulated and increased so as to give a more difficult shot than with live birds themselves. Opportunity is thus afforded to the novice, who can enter the field with a certainty of a measure of success hitherto unheard of, whilst the average man can improve himself in those particular shots in which he is weak.

Brief mention may here be made of a few shots that one is likely to come across at birds other than pheasants and partridges. What man is there that does not feel a thrill of excitement when

he hears the cry of "Mark cock!"? And yet how often when the much-coveted prize comes his way does he miss him "clean" with both barrels.

The woodcock, like the owl and the heron, takes long and slow beats with its wings when flying in the open and appears for this reason to be going more slowly than it really is—hence the shot goes time after time behind. When in covert he is a different bird altogether, and the man who can "snap" him as he zig-zags through the branches of the trees has good reason to be proud of himself.

"MARK 'COCK!"

HOW TO SHOOT. 21

SNIPE.

The snipe, too, is an "erratic" bird. You must be quick if you would bag him, or he is soon out of range; albeit, there are some who prefer to wait till he has finished his gyrations before pulling the trigger, but the wisdom of this proceeding is doubtful for the reason above stated. The landrail is not a very sporting bird, but he is a welcome addition to the bag in September. He is in reality an easy bird to shoot, as he generally flies straight ahead. Still, he can be missed, and good shots have done it, for the simple reason that he looks so easy, and is, like the woodcock in the open, going faster than he appears to be.

Want of space forbids the further extension of these brief notes on shooting, but, in conclusion, let it be impressed once again upon the reader that to shoot well three things are necessary. First, a perfectly-fitting gun; secondly, the best ammunition that money can buy; and, lastly, plenty of practice.

BADMINTON LIBRARY: "A best London gun is somewhat superior as regards strength and excellence of shooting, but it is immensely superior in finish and general appearance, as well as in its balance."

To obtain good shooting, use good cartridges.

GUN-FITTING.

EXAMPLES.

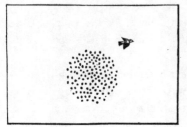

No. 1.—Gun not sufficient "cast-off," and too much bend in stock.

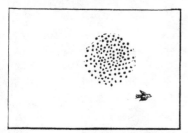

No. 2.—Gun-stock too straight, and not enough "cast-off."

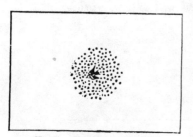

No. 3.—Gun Correct "fit."

For anyone to shoot at his best, it is necessary that the gun should be a good fit; that is to say, when the gun is handled and mounted in the act of shooting, the gun should be so shaped and made as to naturally follow the eye and freely cover the object aimed at, for, however excellent a gun may be, if it is a misfit it is of little use to its owner.

SCIENCE OF GUN-FITTING.

It is more particularly within the last few years that the science of gun-fitting has been brought to perfection. Previous to the invention and general adoption of the try-gun, the eye and judgment of the gunmaker, exercised in his shop, were his only guides in building guns to fit his customers, while the latter were able to test the shooting qualities as regards pattern and penetration only. These haphazard methods were very unsatisfactory to the shooter himself, as well as to his gunmaker. Bad shots

GUN-FITTING.

might go on perseveringly year after year, firing away thousands of cartridges without improvement in their shooting form, simply because the origin of the evil remained undiscovered, because the guns had not been built to suit the personal characteristics of their owners and it was impossible for them to make good shooting with them. The fault often rests, not with the shooters, but in their guns, and, until the real source of error was discovered, constant practice only tended to drive gunners to despair of ever improving in marksmanship. Some gunmakers might be quicker than others in stumbling upon the proper construction of guns to suit the personal peculiarities and requirements of their clientele, but at best it was very much a matter of chance until the try-gun came into use—a marvellous aid in capable hands to discovering the best shape of stock for the individual gunner, and consequently showing up the weak points of a misfitting gun, so that they might be remedied and its shooting improved.

SPECIALISTS.

A gun-fitter or shooting expert should be a specialist in his particular line quite as much as in any other calling; it should be borne in mind that he is not the manufacturer of the gun, but is the individual who ascertains the right shape and style of gun to suit any particular shooter, and should also be able to show that same shooter how best to use the gun when so made.

TRY-GUN.

A sportsman who is a "born shot," with great natural aptitude,

24 SHOOTING.

will often shoot with almost any gun, but for the majority, or average performers, an expert instructor and a good fitting gun are essential to success.

Going a little further into the mysteries of gun-fitting and the making of a crack shot, one may make certain that, whether by painstaking measurements or by fortunate accident, the gun-stock of every sportsman should fit him to a nicety, should he wish to shoot at his best. In the same way persistently bad shooting, where the natural facilities of eyesight, nerve, and strength are fairly good, can, in nine cases out of ten, be traced by an experienced gun-fitter, the fault being in the construction of the stock or boring of the barrels of the gun or in some peculiarity of the sportsman. It may be that the stock is too straight or too bent, too long or too short, too cast off or too cast on, or not enough of either, or too little cast off at the face, the heel, or the toe.

FAULTS MAY BE REMEDIED.

These faults will have to be remedied before the owner can expect to derive benefit from the tuition of a skilled instructor in shooting. These points are determined by the use of the adjustable try-gun in the hands of the shooter at the targets, under the eye of an experienced and closely observant "fitter." By the ingenious use of screws, hinges, and levers, any part of the stock of the try-gun can be altered at will in a few seconds, so as to make the stock an exact copy of any shape possible in a breech-loader of the present day.

SHOOTING SCHOOLS.

To fully appreciate the work thus performed, let the reader imagine himself as a visitor to such a place as the Blagdon Shooting School, with a try-gun and a "fitter" who is able to decide as to the adjustments required from the shooting shown on a range of iron targets before which he now finds himself. These targets (three in number) extend over some 2,500 square feet of whitewashed iron surface, 150 feet in length, and from 15 feet to 22 feet in height, and the apparatus for testing the shooting capacity of both gun and gunner is of the most ingenious and improved description. The first is an angular target, the two sides sloping away from the centre at almost right angles to each other. Across both wings of this target from the centre are sent flying,

FITTING—RIGHT AND LEFT SHOTS.

to right and left, imitation birds at constantly increasing speed and in a gradually rising direction as in natural flight. The highly ingenious mechanism is worked from the covered screen at the centre, which conceals an assistant trained to the work. The breaking of the birds is instantly shown by the disappearance of the black clay on the breast of each, the pattern of the shot being produced on the whitewashed target

FITTING—ELEVATION.

behind. Right and left shots can here be practised to perfection, and by their aid the "fitter" is able to tell whether the gun is shooting too high or too low. If the shot is thrown with a tendency either

FITTING—RISING BIRD.

28   SHOOTING.

high or low, the try-gun is at once resorted to, and the shooter is
asked to fire away with it at the clay birds as they appear for
an instant or two flying across the target away from the shooter
at an increasing speed up to the target's highest corner.

THE SHOOTING IS SEEN TO IMPROVE.

Shot after shot is being fired, the try-gun being gradually altered
until the shooting is seen to improve. The stock is screwed and
unscrewed, perhaps, in half a dozen places, bent this way and that
by the skilled instructor, until at last it becomes fixed in the precise
position that will best enable the shooter to avoid shooting too
high or too low, but exactly at the proper elevation to hit the bird
every time.

Before this is finally decided, the shooter is asked to fire a few
shots at the second target—a flat one, with large expanse, across
which, from left to right and right to left, fly heavy metal discs on
a set of rails running upwards to the tops of the targets. These
discs have clay birds fixed on to the front of them, and are rapidly
spun by special mechanism behind the protected screen in the centre,
and released at a given moment. The spin carries the discs with the
birds up the inclined rails at a speed, increasing by the construction of the mechanism, until they reach the top of the incline, when
they turn back and run down behind the protected screen to be
again similarly operated on.

These two targets are brought into use to ascertain elevation,
but the shooter may still be shooting too much to the right or to
the left; and to further ascertain the precise form of stock best
suited to his figure and eye, a third target has to be tried—a vertical,
flat one of 22 feet in height and eight feet in breadth, on which
there is one imitation bird rising straight away from the bottom
to the top. On the whitewash of this target the pattern made
by the gun at every shot is plainly visible to the shooter himself.
He, perhaps, finds the bulk of his pellets from the try-gun inclined
to hit too much to the right of the bird. At once the fitter is
busily altering the screws in the try-gun, so as to get the proper
cast off or cast on. Another trial with the altered stock, and the

GUN-FITTING.

pellets may perhaps be seen finding their way a little bit too much to the left. Another twist of the screws in the try-gun, and the

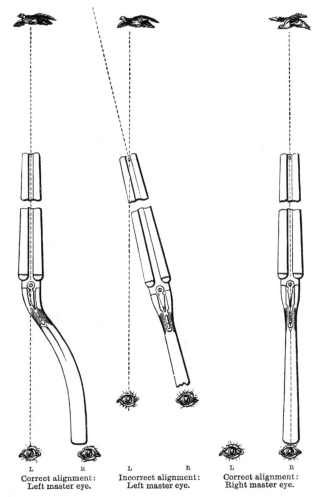

L R	L R	L R
Correct alignment: Left master eye.	Incorrect alignment: Left master eye.	Correct alignment: Right master eye.

position is finally adjusted, so that time after time the shooter is able to plant his charge right on the breast of the rising bird.

THE GUN OF CORRECT SHAPE.

The proper bend of the stock having been ascertained at the first two targets, and its cast off or cast on carefully fixed at the third, an exact copy of the try-gun, as now adjusted, will be the gun with which the shooter should make a good marksman.

ALIGNMENT CONTROLLED BY THE EYE.

The correct alignment of the gun and the object aimed at is controlled by the eye, and one of the most delicate tests of the strength of one eye being stronger than the other is exemplified in aiming with the gun.

THE MASTER EYE.

Shooting from the right shoulder, and the right eye being the master or stronger of the two, the alignment of the gun will be correct if an imaginary line from the eye to the object aimed at passes through the centre of the breech and muzzle of the gun; but, supposing that the left eye is the stronger of the two, the muzzle will be drawn over to the left and intersect a line drawn from the left eye to the object aimed at; consequently, the direction of fire would in this case be to the left of the mark. (See page 29.)

Few shooters indeed have equal sight, one eye or other having the control, and as such the cast-off of the gun will be more or less affected.

THE LEFT EYE THE STRONGER.

When the left eye is the complete master, it means that the sportsman should shoot from the left shoulder, or have a cross-eyed gun, or block the left eye, such as holding the left hand so as to intercept that organ seeing the muzzle of the gun. As to which of these means should be adopted depends a good deal on circumstances, therefore an expert gun-fitter should be consulted.

CROSS-EYED GUN

MODERN GUNS.

THE forerunner of the modern double-barrel gun was the "Le fau cheux," having a drop barrel, with lever fastening, and using

LEVER OVER GUARD GUN.

a pin-fire cartridge; this, in due course, was followed by the lever being placed over the guard and continued into the days of the

TOP-LEVER GUN.

central fire cartridges and rebounding locks. An improvement on this somewhat slow form of opening and closing the gun was the top-lever action.

HAMMERLESS GUNS.

The gun of to-day has a hammerless action, namely, the hammers are inside and cocked by the opening of the gun for loading.

HAMMERLESS GUN.

The principle of this highly-successful gun was introduced over twenty years ago, during which time it has been subjected by leading sportsmen to the most crucial tests in different parts of the world. It can be thoroughly recommended as a well-tried gun.

EJECTOR GUNS.

To the hammerless action is added fired cartridge ejecting mechanism, various methods being employed for that purpose; one of the most successful is here shown. Introduced to the public in 1888, since which date many thousands have been made and sold, it is described by Sir R. Payne-Gallwey, Bart., in the Badminton Library on Shooting, as follows:—

MODERN GUNS.

We have tried one of Messrs. Cogswell and Harrison's ejector guns lately, and it has stood a good deal of rough work, and acted very well; it certainly deserves our praise. It is very simple in construction. There is not a single extra limb or alteration in the lock work of this gun that is caused by its ejecting mechanism. Two sears are hinged on the forepart, the one end controlling the propelling rods, which are placed in a metal box. After firing, the engagement takes place, and the rods are held back until the gun is opened to the extracting position, when, by an ingenious movement of the sear, the rods are released and spring forward, thereby jerking out the exploded cases. It appears to us that not the least important part of this arrangement is that the cartridge is, in any case, extracted the usual distance, and therefore the force required to finally eject it is reduced to a minimum. This fact, of course, adds considerably to the smooth working of the gun.

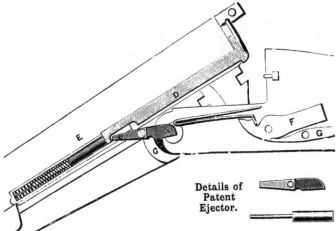

Details of Patent Ejector.

SINGLE-TRIGGER GUN.

The latest innovation acknowledged as an improvement to the hammerless self-ejecting gun is the substitution of one trigger in place of two. Various means have been adopted to effect this end, one example being illustrated, the first model of which was described by the Editor of the "Field," on March 26, 1898, as follows:—

Messrs. Cogswell and Harrison have perfected a new single trigger mechanism which they have had in use for some time past, and, according to their account, it has never been known to fail. The mechanism is of the simplest possible character. It consists of a piece marked "C" in the accompanying woodcut, which is moved back by the backward motion of the bolt when opening the gun. The motion sets the right hand side tumbler in proper position for firing the right barrel. After the discharge of the right barrel, the tumbler has to move round about ninety degrees to the arc of a circle, and is then ready to fire the left barrel. The tumbler, instead of being free to turn almost instantly from the right to the left hand trigger, is caught in the serrated timer (B), and is therefore not free to fire the left hand barrel until the vibration set up by firing the right barrel has entirely ceased.

THE COST OF A GUN.

The cost of a best London-made gun is about £60, or a little more, and such a gun cannot be too highly recommended, as it is an

DETAILS OF SINGLE-TRIGGER GUN.

embodiment of highest quality, perfect design, handiness, finish, and is specially suitable for a great deal of hard work. Furthermore, one cannot do better than take to heart the following extract from the Badminton Library:—

THE SUPERIORITY OF A BEST GUN.

A best London gun is somewhat superior as regards strength and excellence of shooting, but it is immensely superior in finish and general appearance, as well as in its balance.

An ordinary quality gun, with plainer finish, costs about £40 to £50, whilst for those sportsmen not doing a lot of heavy shooting a serviceable gun, with all the latest improvements, such as single-trigger, self-ejector, and such like, can be obtained for about £20 to £30; but for less money the purchaser must sacrifice the single-trigger movement, and for less still the self-ejector.

Never allow the muzzle of your gun to point at anyone—loaded or not.

BORES AND WEIGHTS.

The bore par excellence for game shooting in this country is 12; the average sportsman will make a better bag and cleaner kills

MODERN GUN.

with this than with any other size, but for early in the season, or where weight is a consideration, the smaller bores may be used with advantage. A very great point to be observed is the distribution of weight in a gun, for two guns may weigh the same, balance identically at a corresponding point, have the same length of barrels and stock, and yet handle and feel very differently; the reason being that metal and wood are differently distributed.

An average 12-bore should weigh about 6lb. 10oz. to shoot $1\frac{1}{16}$oz. shot and a suitable charge of smokeless powder; a light model (28in. barrels) for 1oz. shot should be about 6lb.; whereas for a full game charge of $1\frac{1}{8}$oz. a gun of 6lb. 13oz. is advisable. A 16-bore, with 28-in. barrels, weighs about 6lb., and shoots 1oz. shot. A 20-bore, for $\frac{3}{4}$oz. shot and with barrels of the same length, would be lighter; whilst a 28-bore, for $\frac{5}{8}$oz. shot, would be in the neighbourhood of 5lb. 8oz.

Of course, guns can be made lighter than the foregoing weights, but they are apt to jump, and, consequently, not such steady shooting is obtainable.

GUN BARRELS.

The material now almost universally used in barrels is steel, and, if of good quality, is far better than its old rival—Damascus, a mixture of iron and steel. No doubt the latter looks very pretty

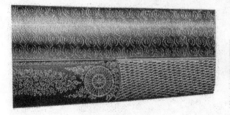

DAMASCUS BARRELS.   STEEL BARRELS.

when nicely browned, distinctly showing the two metals. A mild ductile steel is the requisite for shot-gun barrels, having great elasticity, and capable of withstanding the continual percussive force of the cartridges fired; with such a metal a barrel is much stronger than when made of twisted or Damascus tubes.

For some years Whitworth was the only kind of steel in the market for this purpose, but to-day there are several eminent firms in Sheffield who supply steel of equal quality.

BARREL TUBE MANUFACTURE.

The steel manufacturer supplies blocks of metal to the barrel maker, who in turn drills a hole from one end to the other; then reamers and bores the inside to dimensions, whilst the outsides are turned, trued, and filed to shape. The gun-barrel tubes, for such they are now, are next proved, and then put together with the necessary lumps, ribs, and such like, ready for the action. Such a process as here described can be seen at the Small Arms Factory (Cogswell and Harrison), near Victoria Station, London. The most

GUN-BARREL BORING.

38 SHOOTING.

interesting part of the process is the drilling of the hole, a little over thirty inches long, through the barrel block, and with a variation of only a few thousandths of an inch.

The barrels having been actioned, they are sent to the proof-house to have the final tests made ; after which, so far as the barrels are concerned, that all important subject to the sportsman—the fine-boring and regulating the shooting—is effected.

A GOOD SHOOTING GUN.

No small degree of skill is here employed, and care of the highest order is exercised so as to obtain a good shooting gun, giving an even distribution of pattern, combined with high velocity and great penetration. The gun is then tested, and, if not quite right, an alteration or alterations are made ; though minute, the result may be considerable. There is a narrow limit of metal to work upon, and so the necessity of great care.

SHOT-GUN PATTERNS.

The standard distance for trying the patterns of guns is forty yards, whilst the target is a circle of which the diameter is thirty inches. A cylinder-bored 12-gauge gun, with $1\frac{1}{8}$oz. No. 6 shot (304 pellets), will give a pattern in such a circle of 120 to 130 ; an improved cylinder, 130 to 145 ; whilst a choke-bore will go up to about 220. A 16-bore pattern, with 1oz. No. 6 shot, would be from 100 to 170 ; a 20-bore, with $\frac{3}{4}$oz. No. 6 shot, from 90 to 150 ; and a 28-bore, with $\frac{5}{8}$oz. No. 6 shot, from 70 to 100. So, therefore, a gun can be made to give any desired pattern between these limits, according to requirements.

THE GAME GUN.

For game shooting, walking up in the early part of the season, and for driving, it is now generally considered that a gun should be bored an improved cylinder.

THE LONG RANGE GUN.

For shooting when long shots are often required, the right should be an improved cylinder, and the left a modified choke ; but for

MODERN GUNS. 39

wildfowl or long range game shooting a more powerful and heavier gun and long cartridges might be employed with advantage, the right barrel being bored modified choke and the left a full choke.

BALL AND SHOT GUNS.

For many years it was the aim of experimenters to produce a gun from which shot or ball could be fired from the same barrel with satisfactory results. Success, more or less, crowned these efforts by the employment of the following methods:—First, the rifling of

BALL AND SHOT GUN.

the tube with deep, sharp-cut grooves, nearly straight, from one end of the barrel to the other; secondly, by plain boring until near the muzzle, and then sharp, deep-cut grooves of a quick spiral; and, thirdly, by shallow, wide grooves, without any sharp corners, the rifling being almost invisible except to the expert eye. There is not any patent in either method, so that it is open for any manufacturer to adopt that system from which he can obtain the best results. Suffice it to say that to-day the third plan is that employed by nearly all of the principal makers. With such a gun the accuracy of the ball up to eighty yards is quite

40   SHOOTING.

equal to that of an express rifle, and nearly so up to one hundred yards; whilst the shot patterns are those of an improved cylinder. The third system gives the least recoil of any.

VARIOUS BORES.

Guns of this type are made in 8-, 10-, and 12-bores, **and** are handier and superior to rifles made in these calibres; they cannot be too highly recommended for use abroad.

SHOOTING AT FIFTY YARDS OF BALL AND SHOT GUN: 10-Bore.

PENETRATION OF SHOT GUN.

Given a properly-bored gun, with barrels well designed, penetration will be found satisfactory; but as the degree of penetration depends so much upon the cartridges, this subject will be found on page 49, under the heading of "Ammunition."

THE PROOF OF GUNS.

The first consideration in any firearm is safety. Bearing this in mind it is essential that the gun is, or should be, made to withstand the strain of whatever ammunition it is intended to employ; the gun should have, in addition, an ample margin of safety.

The tubes of a gun, before being put together, are subjected to a provisional proof, carried out by an authority constituted by

law. They undergo the second, or definitive proof, when the gun has the action fitted to the barrels. It is obligatory on all manufacturers and dealers in firearms in England to see that these tests have been carried out.

NITRO PROOF.

There is a third proof now in existence which is optional, but is highly desirable, as almost its title indicates, namely, the "Nitro Proof," for nearly everyone to-day shoots nitro-compounds out of his gun.

UNDUE RISKS: DANGEROUS EXPERIMENTS.

Guns thus being made and proved to withstand specific pressures, it is essential to the shooter's safety that cartridges should not be used that give excessive strains, for many have been the disasters of people experimenting with unknown, and often new, explosives, giving unknown pressures in the gun. Another source of damage sometimes arises from using cartridges of which the cases, when empty, are longer than the chambers of the gun in which they are fired.

TO PROLONG THE LIFE OF THE GUN.

The usual complement of gun fittings are:—Cleaning rod with interchangeable jag, mop, wire brush (Sir R. Payne-Gallwey pattern), and bristle brush, breech chamber cleaner, pocket cleaner in pouch, extractor, pair of turnscrews, pair of snap caps, oil bottle and oil, tow, vaseline, and two flannel cloths.

CLEANING.

After the day's shooting the gun should have the barrels very thoroughly cleaned out with the cleaning rod and jag, upon which latter is wound sufficient tow to fit the bore of the barrel well, but not so tightly as to require much force to move the rod up and down. Lubrication should then be applied to the tow, and the barrel well wiped out. Repeat this at least twice, being careful to use clean tow

MODERN GUNS. 43

each time. Should there be any difficulty in removing any fouling or leading, the bristle or wire brush should be resorted to. The breech cleaner will then be required, care being taken to give the front of the chamber a good cleaning, as dirt and rust readily collect there, and are not easily discernible. For a final dressing the jag of the cleaning rod must be exchanged for the mop and oil, after which the cloth, with a little oil, should be used to remove all fouling, dirt, and such like from under the extractor, and generally on the outside of the barrels wherever situated; a repetition can then be made with another cloth and oil. Next take the pointer from the bottle and oil with a few drops the hook grips and sides of the lump, also extractor. The stock, action, and forepart should be similarly cleaned to the outside of the barrels, spots of oil being placed by the bottle pointer on the parts of friction, namely the knuckle and bolt. Slightly grease the wood of the stock, for by so doing it becomes more impervious to wet, besides having a better appearance with age.

GOOD OIL AND TOW.

Avoid common tow, which is dusty and often contains particles of foreign substances which are liable to scratch the barrels; also beware of unsuitable or common oil. A little of good quality is all that is required; often a gun is gummed up, particularly the trigger work, with a too liberal allowance of bad lubricant from an oil can.

ANNUAL INSPECTION.

A gun should not be taken to pieces except by an expert, and between the seasons it is desirable to send the weapon to a gun-maker for examination, taking to pieces, and thoroughly cleaning; this may be a small expense, but nothing to be compared with the advantage derived in having the gun kept in good working order, besides removing small dents in the barrel, often imperceptible to the owner thereof until shown.

AMMUNITION.

Central-fire cartridges for some years have been almost exclusively used, pin-fires being to-day an extreme rarity. The change from the one system to the other commenced to have appreciable effect in the middle 'sixties. A more recent change, that is, the use of smokeless instead of black powder, although not so decided, has yet taken place to an enormous extent.

SMOKELESS POWDER.

The first practical smokeless powder was undoubtedly Schultze, to be followed some years after by E.C., Amberite, S.S., Cannonite, Kynoch, Walsrode, Ballistite, and S.G.R., besides a host of others. It must, however, be borne in mind that, although their names have been before the world for periods more or less extended, it by no means follows that they always indicate that the powders are the same at different periods of their existence; for it is not too much to say that all, or nearly all, of the manufacturers have changed their products from time to time—in fact, in some instances, many times—so that it comes to this, that the names of the explosives originally introduced remain constant, whereas the powders are a changing quantity. These alterations have often been the means of improving the products of a particular manufacturer, although at other times it has been a retrograde step. Hence the reason why one year a particular brand of powder has been better than some of its rivals, and perhaps the same or following year the order is entirely reversed.

With all these vacillations, however, there has been a great advance in the standard of excellence of smokeless powder, which fact reflects great credit upon the chemists and manufacturers of sporting powders for their arduous and difficult labours. The admitted variability of smokeless powders cannot be contested by anyone having other than a small experience of the subject. To obtain more uniform results, the method of blending several batches of powders is resorted to; of course, this mixture is mechanical, not chemical.

CARTRIDGE CASES.

Cartridge cases are made of brass heads, etc., with paper tubes, and, in the days of black powder, the colour of the latter were green, blue, and brown, and indicated three different qualities; but to-day no such distinction exists; various qualities there are, but colour is no indication. The ordinary paper cases, as made by English manufacturers, are all sufficient for dry weather, but should it be wet the sportsman has the option of paper cases made waterproof with such substances as paraffin, celluloid, etc., or the paper tube of the cartridge case may be had covered with brass.

Great differences of opinion have existed between gun and cartridge makers as to what sizes gun chambers and cartridges should be, but, happily, so far as 12-bores are concerned, there is now a chance of all coming to one mind, as, through the Gunmakers' Association, a common standard for guns and cartridges is about to be fixed, and when such is done no doubt other bores will follow suit, as, although they are not so much in vogue as the 12.'s, the divergencies are far greater.

The cap of the cartridge is all-important, as slight differences therein have important results when used with smokeless powders — very far greater, indeed, than when employed for igniting the older black explosive. The

CAP TESTER.

SHOOTING.

cap composition should be suited to that particular powder it is intended to be used with, otherwise there may arise hang-fires, miss-fires, excessive strain on the gun, attended, perhaps, with serious results, let alone ineffective shooting. Needless to say, the caps should be uniform in result.

CAP TESTING.

The " Cap Tester," an instrument used by many of the leading makers of powder and ammunition in this country, America, France, and Germany can be seen at work at the factory of its makers, namely, Cogswell and Harrison, Limited. This instrument treats the cap as a cartridge, and measures to the most minute degree the force of explosion, as well as the force necessary to explode the cap.

WADS.

Wads should be uniform in texture and in size, both diameter and thickness. The wadding between the powder and shot should be a felt, with a hard wad each side, and over the shot a cardboard; the thickness and kind must depend on the particular issue and quantity of powder used, as well as the weight of shot.

SHOT.

Shot should be spherical and uniform in size, one pellet compared with another. Soft shot is preferable for use on game, as when eaten, no damage to the teeth need be feared. Chilled shot is very hard, and generally used in pigeon shooting.

The following is a table of sizes of shot to 1oz. avoirdupois weight:—

SSG	13	1	104	*6	300
BBB	50	2	120	7	345
BB	58	3	140	8	450
B	75	4	170	9	580
AAA	37	5	220	10	985
AA	40	$5\frac{1}{2}$	240	12	1,760
A	45	6	270	Dust	2,600

* Northern size.

AMMUNITION.

Having dealt with the material to load cartridges, it now comes to see which are the necessary ways of testing that material so as to obtain the maximum efficiency of shooting.

POWDER PRESSURES.

First comes the cap tester, as described on page 46, then, having ascertained certain particulars of the cap and decided what weight and size of shot it is required to shoot, the cartridge is loaded and placed in a crusher gauge to investigate the strain on the gun; if too excessive, the charge of powder must be reduced or the wads changed in kinds or sizes, or the amount of turnover reduced. Should the pressure, however, not be excessive, the velocity of the shot will then be taken; but, before doing so, it will be advisable to briefly describe the

CRUSHER GAUGE.

The crusher gauge is an instrument made internally the same as a gun barrel; a firing mechanism, with breech-piece, is fitted to the rear, movable plugs are situated along the barrel at distances of 1in., 2½in., 5½in., and so on. Upon the head of the plug a lead cylinder is placed, which latter is crushed by the powder gases generated upon the discharge of the cartridge—the greater the strain, the greater the compression. The lead is then measured, and the reading compared with a table to translate the result into tons per square inch.

The Editor of the "Field," on May 6, 1893, wrote on this subject as follows:—

> In no branch of sport has the aid of science been called in to a greater extent than in connection with shooting, and the instruments which have been employed and the experiments which have been made of recent years could never have been dreamed of by the old school of shooting men. To go no further than the invention of the new powders, a life of observation would be necessary to test their respective merits had they to be decided by the gun alone; but by employing a crusher gauge, a representation of which is given herewith, much valuable information is obtained in a single day.
>
> Crusher gauges, as our readers are no doubt aware, are instruments used for ascertaining the pressures given by gunpowder exploded in the barrel of a gun. These gauges have been used for many years by artillerists, and, although it is not pretended that the pressure of

48   SHOOTING.

any given powder in a gun is recorded with absolute mathematical accu-

CRUSHER GAUGE.

racy, the results given are very near the exact truth. The great advantage, however, of using these gauges is the facility with which

AMMUNITION. 49

the pressure given by one gunpowder may be compared with that given by other powders, and also the pressure given by the same powder under different atmospheric and other conditions.

Messrs. Cogswell and Harrison have for many years used crusher gauges, acting on precisely the same principle as here set forth, and they invariably test nitro powder supplied to them. To this fact, no doubt, much of the success which has attended their cartridge-loading business must be attributed.

PENETRATION.

Great as the advance has been in testing the disruptive force on the gun by means of crusher gauges, equally great has been the advance in means for testing penetrative force. Formerly the only tests available for anyone to try the penetrative force of a gun were such as firing against an old tin canister, or an old book and counting the leaves pierced, but the results were very clumsy, and practically of very little service indeed.

If not the first, certainly one of the earliest recognised tests was the Pettit pad, made of forty sheets of brown paper sewn together at the corners; its faults were that penetration depended upon the tightness of the stitching, the slightest difference in the thickness of paper, and its dryness; each of these defects was quite sufficient to place a moderate shooting gun or cartridge before one giving first-class results.

The Pettit pad was followed by the field force gauge, and consisted of a target which retreated when struck by the shot; this instrument was of great service in its day.

The penetration rack was another method, and consisted of a box with sheets of straw board, divided with wood frames, the whole being tightly screwed together by means of a handle at the back; all that can be said of this is that it was on the Pettit pad principle, but without many of its faults.

VELOCITIES.

The electric chronograph to-day alone holds the field, having surpassed all its competitors for exactitude of reading and reliability of results. It is nearly the same set of apparatus as used for artillery. Briefly described, it consists of two separate electric circuits,

E

50   SHOOTING.

with an electro magnet to each. The wire of one current passes near to and in front of the gun to be tested, whilst the wire of the other or second current is fixed to an iron target at a definite distance from the gun, say, thirty feet. Upon firing the cartridge the shot breaks the wire just in front of the muzzle, then traverses the intervening thirty feet of space and strikes the target, the force of the blow making disjunction by means of the contact breaker situated at the back of the iron target.

Each of the before-mentioned electro magnets supports an iron rod when the circuit is closed; but, of course, the rod falls when the current is broken, as the electro magnet has not any longer the power to hold it up. Such is the effect when the gun is fired; first the wire at the muzzle is broken and allows the rod to fall, the second circuit is then broken at the target, and so the electro magnet of this circuit permits its rod to fall, and, in so doing, strikes the sear of a lock, the hammer of which makes a mark on the first rod. Measuring the distance of the drop of the first rod to the mark made by the lock of the second, the time can be ascertained, as both rods fall under the force of gravity.

Instead of employing two rods, a moving plate or drum may be employed, the electro magnets working in conjunction with pens or pointers, which mark the plates or drums, that have previously been blackened with smoke, so as to readily allow of the marks being seen. The plates or drums are moved at definite known speed, or speeds that can be otherwise ascertained by other apparatus.

There are many other details necessary to be known and acted upon in the different kinds of instruments, including the means of firing the gun, which is also done by electricity.

Numerous forms of chronographs have been made, but the broad principle remains the same. The extreme accuracy ascertainable is of the highest order; to-day it is practically the test for penetration carried out by one and all of the leading manufacturers of sporting explosives, cartridge makers, and a few gunmakers. This alone should convince anyone that there is not anything else to compare with such an apparatus for such a purpose; in fact, every gunmaker and cartridge-loader ought to have one.

Having briefly described means whereby the penetration can

AMMUNITION. 51

be reckoned by means of the more advanced method of taking the velocities, it is now necessary to revert to the point where the cartridges were so loaded that the pressures were not excessive, and with this ammunition observe the velocities, which, if too low, will require an alteration of the wadding, or an increase of powder, or a change of cartridge case having a different cap, but after such alteration the pressures should again be taken, so as to be sure the strain is not excessive.

PATTERNS.

There now only remains the pattern on the target, which must be regular and not patchy in its distribution. This subject is dealt with elsewhere.

RECOIL.

The recoil of a gun is ascertained by means of a machine rest, invented by Mr. H. Phillips, of the "Field" newspaper. There have been two models constructed, both of which work admirably, and show comparative recoil of gun and cartridges.

A STANDARDISED CARTRIDGE.

The great desiderata in a standardised cartridge are low pressures, low recoil, good velocity, even pattern, quick ignition, and slow combustion of the powder. Very high patterns are often obtained at the sacrifice of velocity, whilst excessive velocity will so disintegrate the body of shot that wild patterns are the result, and the foremost pellets will be very far in advance of the main body of the charge. Particularly is this so in a very quick combustion powder.

In a cartridge so standardised the velocity should, as far as possible, be kept uniform, no matter what powder or shot is used, as thereby the sportsman's allowance and time would not be affected.

HANG-FIRES.

To ascertain the absence or otherwise of hanging fire, the chronograph is invaluable. It is comparatively easy to find out the time occupied from the moment when the hammer of the gun strikes

E 2

52   SHOOTING.

the cap of the cartridge to the moment when the shot leaves
the muzzle of the gun, or, in fact, any point in the barrel.

The "Field" of December 4, 1886, reported the following experiments as to hang-fires : —

> It will doubtless also interest many of our readers to know the
> amount of time which elapses between the fall of the hammer and the
> departure of the shot from the barrel.   Mr. Griffith has had very great
> experience in this class of experiment to ascertain whether there is any
> tendency to hang fire, and, if such should be found to be the case, means
> are taken to remedy it.
>
> The gun used for this purpose is a 12-bore C.F., choked. Using
> the standard charge of 3 drs. powder and 1⅛ oz. shot, with ordinary
> cartridge case and cap, the time, taken by chronograph, from the ham-
> mer falling to the shot reaching the muzzle of the gun averaged .0077
> of a second with black powder (C. and H. No. 4), and with Schultze
> powder the average was .0096 of a second. With 12-bore pin-fire cases
> the times are slightly less than those previously stated, owing, no
> doubt, to there being no brass dome between cap and powder to ob-
> struct the flash. With large, strong caps, the time was reduced with
> the black to .0070, and with Schultze to .0080 of a second. With
> basket powder the time was shorter than with No. 4, being only
> .0064 of a second; and with No. 6 it was longer, being .0090 of a
> second.
>
> With larger bores than 12-gauge, and also with larger charges in the
> 12-bore gun, the times are, as a rule, slightly longer than stated above.
> With smaller bores than 12, the times are slightly less, unless the gun
> is heavily choked.
>
> When the time taken exceeds .03 of a second, it is distinguished as a
> perceptible hang-fire on the gun being fired from the shoulder; and
> when the time taken exceeds .06 of a second, a "click" is heard be-
> tween the pulling of the trigger and the report of the discharge.

GUN STRIKERS.

The cause of a hang-fire may be in the gun having its striker
too short, as shown in the "Field" of April 10, 1897, wherein a
gun was employed with varying lengths of strikers, as follows: —

1. Full length (0·100 inch)   ...   .   Blunt
2.   ,,   ,, ...   Sharp
3. Three-quarter length (0·075 inch)   ...   .   Blunt
4.   ,,   ,, ...   Sharp
5. Half length (0.050)   ...   .   Blunt
6.   ,,   ,, ...   Sharp
7. One-quarter length (0·025 inch)   ...   .   Blunt
8.   ,,   ,, ...   Sharp

With each varying length and alteration of shape experiments
were conducted, the following, amongst other results, being obtained : —

AMMUNITION. 53

WITH BLUNT STRIKERS.

No.	Shortest	Times of Ignition Longest	Difference	Velocity Ft. sec.
1	·0045	·0064	·0019	1,226
3	·0049	·0060	·0011	1,208
5	·0052	·0110	·0058	1,189
7	·0055	·0167	·0112	1,205 (4 misfires)

WITH SHARP-POINTED STRIKERS.

2	·0054	·0073	·0019	1,212
4	·0047	·0084	·0037	1,190
6	·0058	·0138	·0080	1,191
8	All misfires			

For it is beyond question that the same caps will not answer equally well for all explosives, and a modification in the internal form of the cartridge case and the chemical nature of the detonating composition will produce different effects on different nitro-compounds. But one fact may be relied upon, viz., that whatever the caps and whatever the powders, the best results are not likely to be obtained if defective springs and strikers with bad points are used to ignite them. Moral: Use blunt points in preference to sharp ones if you wish to get the best results out of your cartridges; and never let your guns go too long without sending them to the makers, with the view of getting the strikers restored to good working order. If the strikers are of proper length, they will produce tolerably good results, even with the weaker caps.

SHOT VELOCITIES FOR GIVEN DISTANCES.

To demonstrate how differences of caps affect smokeless powders, the " Field " conducted some experiments, and reported thereon on March 21, 1896.

Three kinds of powder were taken and marked A, B, and C; these were fired with two kinds of cartridges, marked X, Y. The results show how necessary it is to give the cartridge loader a free hand as to cap and powder, or, preferably, both.

					Cartridges	30-inch Barrels Velocity: Ft. Sec.
A powder	...	...	...	...	X cases	1,113
,,	...	...	...	...	Y cases	1,136
B powder	...	...	...	...	X cases	1,106
,,	...	...	...	...	Y cases	1,135
C powder	...	...	...	...	X cases	1,110
,,	...	...	...	...	Y cases	1,150

The following two tables from the " Field " of December 4, 1886, show the velocities given by different sizes of shot for the distances stated : —

54 SHOOTING.

POWDER, 3 Drs. (−42 Grs.) ; Shot, 1 oz.

Size of Shot.	5 yds.	10 yds.	15 yds.	20 yds.	25 yds.	30 yds.	35 yds.	40 yds.	45 yds.	50 yds.	55 yds.	60 yds.
1	1,185	1,168	1,150	1,120	1,076	1,039	992	939	919	880	852	831
2	1,178	1,160	1,139	1,109	1,060	1,016	970	920	882	856	831	804
3	1,168	1,146	1,120	1,094	1,051	999	956	906	876	846	810	779
4	1,162	1,137	1,117	1,081	1,040	982	940	892	855	822	794	758
5	1,160	1,133	1,106	1,066	1,021	969	922	879	840	801	764	729
6	1,154	1,130	1,100	1,061	1,012	950	904	862	826	770	730	694
7	1,147	1,122	1,101	1,056	1,004	951	900	846	796	740	690	631
8	1,136	1,116	1,092	1,038	978	928	866	820	782	730	665	590
9	1,123	1,101	1,080	1,031	961	914	839	790	749	685	603	520
10	1,120	1,094	1,071	1,029	959	891	809	751	704	630	559	440

POWDER, 3 Drs. (−42 Grs.) ; Shot, 1⅛ oz.

Size of Shot.	5 yds.	10 yds.	15 yds.	20 yds.	25 yds.	30 yds.	35 yds.	40 yds.	45 yds.	50 yds.	55 yds.	60 yds.
1	1,169	1,140	1,126	1,089	1,054	1,006	962	935	914	891	861	825
2	1,160	1,128	1,110	1,080	1,041	982	950	918	881	856	820	790
3	1,153	1,118	1,091	1,064	1,033	973	935	899	867	837	798	745
4	1,134	1,106	1,088	1,064	1,020	964	925	887	849	808	759	706
5	1,127	1,034	1,070	1,047	1,014	970	914	875	835	790	741	672
6	1,119	1,091	1,063	1,035	999	942	890	850	808	769	717	652
7	1,091	1,069	1,042	1,008	964	919	866	820	780	737	686	617
8	1,083	1,056	1,026	981	935	885	835	786	739	689	626	556
9	1,080	1,050	1,006	957	906	861	815	750	683	614	535	450
10	1,076	1 041	999	941	886	831	775	710	540	465	480	375

REMAINING SHOT VELOCITIES.

The velocities just given are for stated distances, although lower for any increase of range, but the table does not show the remaining velocity at the end of the given range, as will be seen on reference to the following tables from the "Field," of May 12, 1888, and October 31, 1891 :—

MEAN AND ACTUAL VELOCITIES WITH 1⅛ oz. No. 6, and 3 Drs. POWDER.

Mean velocities for different full ranges.		Mean velocities for separate 5 yards.		Estimated actual velocities.
Range. Yards.	Feet per second.	Yards.	Feet per second.	Feet per second.
5	1 111	First 5	1,111	1,111 (at 2½ yards).
10	1,079	5 to 10	1,049	1,080 at 5 yards.
15	1,044	10 ,, 15	980	1,015 at 10 yards.
20	1 007	15 ,, 20	909	
25	966	20 ,, 25	833	871 at 20 yards.
30	923	25 ,, 30	754	
	881	30 ,, 35	691	723 at 30 yards.
40	840	35 ,, 40	633	
45	800	40 ,, 45	577	605 at 40 yards.
50	758	45 ,, 50	517	
55	708	50 ,, 55	429	473 at 50 yards.
60	647	55 ,, 60	333	

AMMUNITION.

MEAN VELOCITY.

	Muzzle. Ft. sec.	40 yds. Ft. sec.		Muzzle. Ft. sec.	40 yds Ft. sec.
No. 1 shot: 3 drs.	1,154	777	No. 5 shot: 3 drs.	1,111	636
No. 2 shot: 3 drs.	1,145	732	No. 6 shot: 3 drs.	1,103	605
No. 3 shot: 3 drs.	1,128	701	No. 7 shot: 3 drs.	1,095	577
No. 4 shot: 3 drs.	1,119	667	No. 8 shot: 3 drs.	1.087	545

While considering these variations in velocity, it will be well to bear in mind that the killing power of the shot does not vary in the same ratio as its speed. Take, for example, the records for No. 4 shot; the velocity with 3 drs. at 45 yards is very similar to that for 40 yards with 2½ drs., and, the velocity being nearly equal, the striking force would be very nearly alike at their respective distances. But at equal distances there is a marked difference. At 40 yards, for instance, the velocity with 3 drs. is nearly 10 per cent. higher than with 2½ drs.; but the advantage in killing power is not limited to 10 per cent.; as, on calculating out the "energy," or striking force of the shot, it is found that the advantage in this respect is about 21 per cent.; at 45 yards the advantage in velocity is reduced to 7 per cent., while in killing power it amounts to 14½ per cent. And so it follows, as a general rule, that when the velocities of projectiles of equal weight are known, the superiority which one has over another, as regards velocity, may be taken as corresponding with rather more than double that amount of superiority in striking force.

With variations in weight of shot, however, it is rather troublesome to work out the differences; and we therefore give an extract from some tables we calculated for our own use. The figures between parentheses—as (270) after No. 6—show the number of pellets to an ounce of the respective sizes.

ENERGY

ENERGY OF SHOT PELLETS AT DIFFERENT RATES OF SPEED.

Velocity, ft. sc.	1oz. of shot. ft. lb.	No. 4 (174) ft. lb.	No. 5 (218) ft. lb.	No. 5½ (240) ft lb.	No. 6 (270) ft. lb.	No.6½ (300) ft. lb.	Velocity, ft. sc.	1oz. of shot. ft. lb.	No. 4 (174) ft. lb.	No. 5 (218) ft. lb.	No. 5½ (240) ft. lb.	No. 6 (270) ft. lb.	No.6½ (300) ft. lb.
400	156	0·90	0·72	0·65	0·58	0·52	610	364	2·09	1·67	1·52	1·35	1·21
410	164	0·94	0·76	0·68	0·61	0·55	620	376	2·16	1·72	1·57	1·39	1·25
420	172	0·99	0·79	0·72	0·64	0·57	630	388	2·23	1·77	1·62	1·44	1·29
430	181	1·04	0·83	0·75	0·67	0·60	640	400	2·30	1·83	1·67	1·48	1·33
440	189	1·09	0·87	0·79	0·70	0·63	650	413	2·37	1·89	1·72	1·53	1·38
450	198	1·14	0·91	0·82	0·73	0·66	660	426	2·44	1·95	1·77	1·58	1·42
460	207	1·19	0·95	0·86	0·76	0·69	670	439	2·52	2·01	1·82	1·62	1·46
470	216	1·24	0·99	0·90	0·80	0·72	680	452	2·60	2·07	1·88	1·67	1·51
480	225	1·29	1·03	0·94	0·84	0·75	690	465	2·67	2·13	1·94	1·72	1·55
490	234	1·35	1·08	0·98	0·87	0·78	700	479	2·75	2·20	2·00	1·77	1·59
500	244	1·40	1·12	1·02	0·90	0·82	710	493	2·83	2·26	2·06	1·82	1·63
510	254	1·46	1·16	1·06	0·94	0·85	720	507	2·91	2·32	2·12	1·87	1·68
520	264	1·52	1·21	1·10	0·98	0·88	730	521	2·99	2·39	2·18	1·92	1·73
530	274	1·58	1·26	1·14	1·01	0·92	740	535	3·07	2·46	2·24	1·97	1·78
540	285	1·64	1·31	1·19	1·05	0·95	750	549	3·15	2·53	2·30	2·02	1·83
550	295	1·70	1·35	1·23	1·09	0·98	760	564	3·24	2·60	2·36	2·06	1·88
560	306	1·76	1·40	1·27	1·13	1·02	770	579	3·33	2·67	2·42	2·14	1·93
570	317	1·82	1·45	1·32	1·17	1·06	780	594	3·42	2·74	2·48	2·20	1·98
580	328	1·89	1·51	1·37	1·22	1·09	790	609	3·51	2·81	2·54	2·26	2·03
590	340	1·95	1·56	1·42	1·26	1·13	800	624	3·60	2·88	2·60	2·32	2·08
600	352	2·02	1·61	1·47	1·30	1·17							

As the No. 5½ shot is a good deal used, we have thought it might be of interest to include it in the above table, although it was not used in the trial. For larger or smaller sizes, closely approximate estimates may be obtained by taking the records for three sizes smaller or larger, and halving or doubling them, thus:—

No. 1 (94 pellets), double No. 4.　　No. 7 (340 pellets), halve No. 4.
No. 2 (116 pellets), double No. 5.　　No. 8 (448 pellets), halve No. 5.
No. 3 (139 pellets), double No. 6.

There will, of course, be slight variations from strict accuracy in these estimates; but the differences are not nearly so great as occur between shot of the same nominal size issued by different makers.

The use of the Energy table may be readily extended above or below the velocities there stated, by halving or doubling a given number, and multiplying or dividing by four, as being the square of two. Thus, if the energy of a pellet with .250 f.s. be required, take that for 500 and divide by four; or, if one for 1,200 f.s. be sought, take that for 600, and multiply by four. The effect will be similar to what is shown by 400 and 800 in the above table,

AMMUNITION. 57

the number of ft. lbs. in the bottom lines being four times as great as those in the top line. If it should chance that a further extension were required, it may be met by substituting the numbers three and nine for two and four. The result is similar, whether the quantities given in line 750 are divided by nine, or those in line 500 are divided by four; they equally represent the energy for 250 f.s. A combined use of these two tables may be made and applied to ascertain the relative striking force of shot at different distances. Let us suppose that A and B are discussing the respective merits of large and small shot—the former preferring No. 4 and the latter No. 7. It is claimed by B that he has double the chance of hitting his game, because he has twice as many pellets; and A retorts that he does not want to "stuff his bird with atoms of lead," but when he does hit he likes to kill. There is no doubt that B has double the chance of hitting, and this chance he retains, whether the distance is long or short; his pellets, too, may have ample force at short distances, though they never have half so much force as pellets of double their weight. They also lose their force more rapidly, as may be seen from the following comparison, in which are included some short distances not given in the first table:—

Distance. Yards.	No. 4 Shot.		No. 7 Shot.		Proportion of pellet force.
	Velocity. ft. sec.	Energy. ft. lb.	Velocity. ft. sec.	Energy. ft. lb.	
20	909 equal	4·64	838 equal	1·97	2¼ to 1
30	754 ,,	3·19	682 ,,	1·31	2¼ to 1
40	667 ,,	2·58	577 ,,	0·94	2¾ to 1
45	607 ,,	2·07	497 ,,	0·69	3 to 1
50	549 ,,	1·70	405 ,,	0·46	3¾ to 1
55	500 ,,	1·40	324 ,,	0·29	5 to 1

Possibly, too, someone might like to know the total amount of energy in a charge of shot when it leaves the muzzle of the gun, or when it has reached any given distance. Then the second column in the Energy table will enable this to be ascertained for 1oz. of shot, no matter what the size of the pellets may be, or whether it be a bullet; and, if for a charge of other weight, the figures may be increased or diminished in proportion. Supposing, for instance, it is known that the muzzle velocity of a charge is 1,200 f.s., and its remaining velocity at 40 yards is 600 f.s., the amount of energy

58 SHOOTING.

in the former case is rather over 1,400 ft. lb., and in the latter it is rather over 350 ft. lb.; and it will be found that, whenever the velocity is reduced one-half between the muzzle of the gun and the target at 40 yards (and such is about the proportion with small shot), then no less than three-fourths of the energy originally contained in the charge has been expended in overcoming air resistance for that short range.

RATES OF FLIGHT OF BIRDS.

The flights of pigeons, partridges, and pheasants were, in 1887, investigated by Mr. Griffith, and reported in the "Field" of February 19 of that year. The flights were found to be: For good blue pigeons, 13 yards per second, or 27 miles per hour; for partridges, 14 to 15 yards per second, or 30 miles per hour; and for pheasants, 17 yards per second, or 35 miles an hour.

A light breeze of wind amounts to 14 miles an hour, a good steady breeze to 21, whilst a gale is forty; therefore driven birds coming down wind would go considerably faster.

GROUSE SHOOTING.

The remark made that life would be tolerable if it were not for its amusements must have been made in ignorance of the pleasures of grouse shooting. Fishing has its votaries in thousands, and hunting makes life pleasurable for a large number; but neither of them rivals grouse shooting as a healthy and amusing recreation. Expensive though it may be, no other sport obtainable in these islands can be mentioned that so combines in itself all the requisites for the refreshment of a wearied mind and body. Recreation of some kind is as necessary to the well-being of the over-worked business man as to the devotee of London fashionable life. What they both want on an autumn holiday is that resuscitation of mind and muscle which is only obtainable by a thorough change of occupation, ideas, and environment. Walking exercise alone is not of itself sufficiently absorbing to take the mind of a keen stockbroker or merchant from his speculations and books; the author from the prospects of his forthcoming novel or play; the barrister from the contents of his briefs; or the doctor from the ailments of his patients. Though in walking they may be exercising their muscles and deriving physical benefit from the fresh air, giving their whole frames a healthful change, their minds, unless thoroughly educated in things rural, are altogether unrefreshed, perhaps more busily at work than usual concerning the troubles and worries inseparable from every-day life. They may have never learned to read the language in which the book of Nature spread before them is written. The processes of husbandry, the varying vegetation of the seasons, the notes of the birds, the aspect of the hills and skies have not sufficient charm to wean their thoughts entirely from the round of business or the pursuit of pleasures left behind. But in healthful recreation is implied the

60 SHOOTING.

refreshment of mind as well as body; an entire change for both from the beaten track. The most beneficial results cannot be obtained if the one be exercised while the other remains neglected.

POPULARITY OF GROUSE SHOOTING.

It is in this view that grouse shooting has attained the great popularity it enjoys—a popularity that is easily justified. Hard walking is almost unnoticed in the continuous excitement of finding and shooting bird after bird. The bracing air expands the lungs and invigorates the muscles, the dormant instinct of pursuing is aroused, making walking, however arduous in reality, easy to the senses; the brain and eyes are needed to direct and follow the working of the dogs, whilst arms and hands are fully occupied in handling the gun, to be in instant readiness to take advantage of any opportunity that presents itself. In such a day's sport the amount of healthful exercise secured for both body and mind can only be realised when, with a good bag, the sportsman returns home, sufficiently hungry to enjoy a hearty meal, and sufficiently tired to ensure a good night's rest. Grouse shooting may be costly, but it is recreation of the best kind, worth its price in the equivalent acquisition of health, mental and physical, for the battle of life throughout the year.

Grouse shooting, in truth, comes nearer to the idea of wild sport than any other description of shooting. The birds themselves are as wild as the mountains on which they may be sought. Until they rise before the gunners they have been total strangers to the face of man, bred without his aid amidst the heather on the purple hills. The sportsman again cannot help feeling that on the steep mountain-side he is face to face with Nature, untrammelled and uncontrolled, imbued with the unconstrained feelings of enjoyment produced by breathing the bracing mountain air and breasting the towering hills in pursuit of thoroughly wild and wary birds. Given good weather and a fair stock of grouse, there is no more enjoyable mode of spending August than, gun in hand, in pursuit of the birds of the heather, while located in an accessible and luxurious residence, with lovely grounds and beautiful valleys, through which flows, mayhap, a trout or salmon stream. Fin, fur, and feather are

WHEN THE BLISSFUL TWELFTH CAME ROUND.

GROUSE. 63

there, within reach of the keen sportsman during the long autumn days; his table filled with game and fish killed by himself and his friends; before him vast expanses of beautiful moorland, splendid panoramas of mountain and glen, rocky ravines hemming in the rippling streams or roaring gorge, towering heights looking down upon heathered plains and valleys in silence undisturbed by the sight or sound of man. Who does not feel invigorated and refreshed by shooting amid such surroundings, exhilarating and intoxicating as champagne to the senses?

GOING GROUSE SHOOTING.

Going grouse shooting! The words have a pleasant sound as the curtain is rung down upon the season in town, and those meditating an attack upon the grouse are packing up their traps ere starting for Euston, St. Pancras, or King's Cross on their northern journey. Euston for years secured almost the whole of the grouse traffic, but since the opening of the Forth Bridge, King's Cross has obtained an increasing share, St. Pancras having to be content with less. The platforms of any of these three railway stations early in August is worth seeing. Gun cases are seen piled on the top of fishing baskets and mountains of boxes, evidently fashioned for the safe carriage of feminine apparel, dogs are yelping in the dog boxes, now so greatly improved upon the cruel torture chambers to which they were condemned only a few years ago; butlers, grooms, footmen, and ladies' maids are running hither and thither, and all is excitement; till, "Right away!" and their employers steam off to grouse-land. It is a busy scene, but, withal, cannot be compared to that presented to the grouse shooter on his arrival at the railway station, say, of Perth, remarkable for its size, its breakfasts, and the admired confusion that reigns upon its vast arrival platform for the few days before the glorious Twelfth. Dogs are the outstanding feature, their joy at release being expressed by their barking and extravagant capering, which their owners vainly endeavour to quiet. Porters rush along with heavily-laden barrows, keepers in kilts are meeting keepers in velveteens and corduroys to help them with the dogs brought North from English kennels. The platform is littered with heavy ammuni-

64

SHOOTING.

tion and other boxes, through which women, men, and dogs are endeavouring to thread their way, the Scotch accent mingling with the English dialect in strange medley.

Extreme is the contrast between this bustling scene and that presented as the shooter drives up to the quiet and picturesquely situated lodge on the side of the well-wooded valley, the home of the grouse shooting party he is about to join.

ARRIVAL AT THE MOOR.

On the road to the moor, a glorious prospect it is that opens out before him after the first " hill face " is climbed, and the dogs are uncoupled for the morning's work ; gorgeous colouring in the distance, in the fore-ground the well-knit figures of the keepers and gillies, the liver-and-white setters taking their first scamper over the heather. But now the sport is beginning, and all attention must be devoted to it. A few hints to the beginner here may not be out of place. Let us suppose that the beginner finds himself alongside one other gunner who is an adept. The first thing to be carefully noted is the direction of the wind. This must be kept in mind constantly as the dogs are working, for when they are seen to point it is necessary to come to a quick conclusion as to the position of the birds, which can only be decided by observing the wind. A cross wind is the best—that is, a wind blowing across the ground being beaten—and it is advisable to work the higher lying grounds in the forenoon, and the lower stretches towards evening. This, however, will be attended to by the keeper, if he knows his work, and one need only narrowly watch the dogs. When a point occurs on a properly-worked ground, the birds will always be found lying up-wind of the dog, and as soon as he points one should walk immediately in a slanting direction to the ground ahead of his nose. If the dog draws ahead, follow him quickly, as the birds are probably wild and are running before him. A grouse always rises with his breast up-wind, if there be a breeze at all, and the easiest shot is just when he is turning to fly down-wind immediately after rising. To take this shot, one must take care to be quick in throwing the gun up to the shoulder as soon as the bird shows, and not to be awkwardly placed as regards one's

YOU NEVER KNOW WHAT WILL GET UP.

GROUSE. 67

footing on uneven or rough ground as the bird is expected to rise. In the excitement it is difficult to observe obstacles in the path, but it is essential that one should not go stumbling along, or the bird is certain to be missed. Plant your feet firmly on the heather at every step, so that at any time you can shoot from a firm foundation. Take things easily to commence with, remembering that the forenoon is not the best time to make a bag, and that one's strength has to be reserved for the afternoon and the evening, when the birds lie better and the scent is strong. The worst time of the day for shooting is in the heat of the early afternoon sun, and it should be utilised for luncheon in some shady spot near a stream, where an hour's rest is not too much. It is not time wasted, by any means; the dogs and grouse are all the better for it, as well as the keepers and shooters. A good deal, however, depends in more ways than one upon the weather in the regulation of the day's work. In wild, wet weather it is best not to shoot at all, but, if you do, grouse are only to be found in the sheltered locations behind protecting ridges. In fine weather grouse prefer the higher grounds, and have to be attacked there before they can be shot on the lower areas. But on moderately fine days they divide their attention, taking to the higher grounds in the morning and preferring the lower ranges as evening draws near. In the entire absence of wind the ground must be worked more closely, and there is not so much need for care in the manner of beating. But, in grouse shooting as in stalking, a good keeper works entirely by his observation of the wind. By it he can judge where the birds are most likely to be found, and by its aid he is able to interpret the meaning of the movements of his dogs. One must judge for himself as to the pace that is desired in going up to each point, keeping in view that in three cases out of four there is something to be gained by silent swiftness of approach. A steady, well-trained dog should not require a word or even a sign from the keeper to prevent his flushing birds. And many a chance is lost by whistling or shouting to the dogs, particularly in the case of points near the tops of the hillocks, over which the birds are able to run and disappear in safety before the gunners reach the summits. If possible, the dog should be always kept in sight, especially if one cannot absolutely depend on its stanchness.

F 2

68   SHOOTING.

Should he disappear over a ridge, it is worth while following him at once, instead of leaving that duty to the keeper. If the birds are there the keeper's appearance on the sky-line and his directions to the dog are very apt to flush the covey, and the shooter comes up too late even to see them disappear. Promptness in getting to the point in such cases is as advisable as deliberation where birds are about on level ground and there is difficulty in finding them after the covey has been broken. In such cases single birds may be found down-wind of the dog, or the dog may be found puzzling between two broken coveys. The rule is that in cases where delay is likely to be dangerous, the gunner nearest to the point should get up quickly to it, without waiting for his companion or companions. And, in fact, most shooters extend this rule to nine points out of ten, the only exceptions being made where the birds are numerous and tame, the cover ample, and it is desirable to make as large a bag as possible in the shortest space of time. Courtesy and consideration for the failings, if there be any, of your companion in grouse shooting are the marks of a true sportsman. He may be a slow walker or a poor shot, he may be of a highly excitable, nervous temperament or of a lethargic disposition that takes everything for granted, but it is unfair to take advantage of his weaknesses by robbing him of his chances of making his fair share of the bag. Better to sacrifice a few shots that might have come to you by a pushfulness in bag-making than to obtain a reputation for overreaching companion shooters to their annoyance and chagrin. There should be an absolute absence of all jealousy between a pair of grouse shooters if the sport is to be thoroughly enjoyable to all. To this end it is advisable where two parties are out on the moor that the two better and more active shots should be paired together, leaving the two slower and less skilful gunners to keep each other company and to condole with each other when they make mistakes, so that by harmonious working the best results may be realised.

SCOTCH AND ENGLISH MOORS.

There are, of course, great differences of configuration in the grouse moors of Scotland, some of them being as flat as billiard-tables,

BRING THEM DOWN NEATLY AND WELL.

GROUSE. 71

while others are entirely hill faces, with very little level ground on their whole extent. In the north of England there is greater regularity in the moors, and the use of the dogs is more easily dispensed with. Driving is seen at its best on the latter, and before we conclude we may have something to say as regards that mode of shooting "the birds of the heather." But on the great majority of Scotch moors the shooter would be very much at sea without his dog until the birds begin to get very wild and wary, when driving is resorted to. As long as the dogs used are well-broken, well-exercised, and in good condition, it is a matter of fancy whether one employs pointers or setters. If the ground be easy and comparatively level, pointers may be preferable, as they do the neater work. But for other moors, again, where hills are steep and the ground rougher and more extensive, the wide-ranging setter is the more satisfactory for many reasons, chief of these being his stamina, his thickness of coat, strength of feet, and rapidity of movement. He will do twice the work in the course of the day that the pointer could get through, and as long as the moor is well watered, so that he can easily quench his thirst, will go on working day after day, if need be, for weeks without an interval of rest, though few sportsmen require to put him to that extreme test. If he is inclined to be a little wild at the commencement of the season, he loses all that as it progresses, improving with every day's shooting he goes through, let the weather be what it may. Steady and well handled, it is interesting to watch the movements of a pair of good setters, and the shooter would do well not to attempt to control their work. Each dog has its own peculiarities, and many of them will only work heartily for their keepers; the more interference by the gunners the less satisfactory the results. But every movement of the dog has to be closely watched by the gunner, and each bit of ground has to be studied if a good bag of game is to be made. Forty brace of grouse to two guns per day is regarded as a good bag over dogs; thirty brace is a fair one. As the season advances, the bags that can be made over the dogs naturally decrease day by day, until the time comes when it is difficult to get near the birds, which begin to pack, rising wildly at the distant approach of a shooting party long before the dogs have got within scenting distance.

DRIVING.

It is here that driving comes in useful on moors that are more or less fitted for its adoption, and, as it is the rule on many English moors from beginning to end of season, we may give a few hints concerning it, equally applicable to both countries. There are, of course, difficulties connected with driving in Scotland that are not to be found in England. These proceed from the unfavourable nature of the ground on most Scotch shootings, and the impossibility of obtaining a sufficient number of drivers in the less populated country. The Scotch harvest is always late, and in sparsely inhabited districts the inhabitants are engaged during every fine day during the autumn in securing their crops. But, given a sufficiency of drivers and a tolerably level moor, driving can be adopted in Scotland with successful results. Inequalities in the conformation of a moor do not necessarily bar driving; they can even be turned to account by those accustomed to study their ground with this object. But to do this the habitual flights of birds have to be closely observed, as they generally fly by the same route when disturbed in basking or feeding. To pass over the rocky ridges they invariably select the same passes, and by placing the butts just behind these ridges on the tracks usually taken by the birds, good results are always obtainable as the birds come flying through the passes with the wind and vanishing over the ridges. Possibly the moor embraces two sides of a valley, the bottom of which is cultivated ground. The birds prefer in such circumstances to fly along the hill-side they have been disturbed on to crossing the valley to the other side, and an observant keeper can easily place his butts on the line he has often observed them adopt. A study of the routes they take is all that is necessary for successful driving on the hill-sides, and if the birds are found travelling too high above the butts it is a sign that the latter are wrongly placed, not that the moor cannot be driven. By changing the batteries nearer to the alighting places of the birds, they can certainly be bagged. A skilful keeper will make experimental drives until he discovers the proper places for his butts, which should always be selected just

UPWARDS AND OVER THE GUNS.

GROUSE. 75

behind the ridge or sky-line, so as to give the gunners about fifty yards in front to observe the approach of the grouse. The more the butts are concealed from the birds, the larger are likely to be the bags. The best sport is invariably found where one cannot perceive the flight of the birds from long distances, but only when coming right on to the batteries. The great authority on driving, Mr. A. I. Stuart Wortley, maintains that the distance from butt to ridge should in no case exceed eighty yards, giving just time to get ready, to select your bird, and to get your gun up before the birds are over the butts. Mr. Stuart Wortley has given most elaborate directions as to the placing of the butts and the management of drives. But we may assume that these have been attended to by our host and his keepers, with the best results, and our grouse driver arrives on the ground and draws lots for his butt, which, gun in hand, he proceeds to occupy. Taking his place in the centre, the loader crouches down on the left, beside him his bag of cartridges well open on the seat. The shooter puts a few cartridges in his right-hand coat pocket, in case of accident, and leans his pair of loaded guns against the front of the butt, which should be just high enough to shoot over comfortably when he is upright. The drivers are advancing in horse-shoe formation, with good flanking, and presently their flags appear in the distance over the ridge. It is now time to take up the gun, for the birds may soon appear; there they are coming along, the first pack off the flank of the drive. They are all old birds, wary cocks, that get up in advance to make sure of escape. Bang! and the first one goes down. Bang! and the second follows. A still sharper watch has now to be kept, as the birds flying over the heather are not easily seen against the ground. There are a dozen of them sailing along. Another brace fall to the right and left, and the second gun drops a third stone dead as they swing back together, giving to the nearest butt a chance of which its occupant is not slow to avail himself. The birds now keep coming over more frequently, and one's work is cut out for him in running his eyes all over the ground in front of him from right to left and back again. One has to keep cool, though it is difficult to do so, particularly when the large packs come streaming over the butts, and one gets seven or eight barrels

76   SHOOTING.

into them before they are out of range. Misses will be made, counter-
balanced, however, by numerous good kills.

THE BEST PERFORMERS.

The best performers go on shooting without turning, so long
as birds keep coming towards them, selecting the easiest shots in
quick succession. Where three birds come over a few seconds of time
are gained by leaving the left barrel of the first gun undischarged
and dropping the second and third birds with the second gun. As
the drivers approach within 150 yards or so, one has to shoot more
carefully, avoiding straight shots low in front and selecting high
or side birds. A few more double shots, and the drivers showing
all along the line give evidence that the drive is over, and the
" pick up " can be begun. In this the shooter has to assist with
his gun, taking care to shoot at a bird should it show signs of escaping
only where there is no chance of damaging a beater. And so one drive
is succeeded by another until the end of the day.

If the marksmanship required for shooting grouse over dogs,
particularly during the early weeks of the season, is comparatively
easy, it has to be added that the shooting of driven grouse with
accuracy and effect is unsurpassed for difficulty in the whole range
of game shooting. The " endless variety of angle, curve, elevation,
and pace in the flight of driven grouse," as Mr. Stuart Wortley de-
scribes it, accounts for the undoubted fascination grouse driving
exerts over the minds of crack game shots, as well as for the
difficulty in its mastery by the novice. Practice alone can give perfection in it, and we merely hint that, as a rule, the novice is apt
to shoot below rather than above his birds, and before rather than
behind them. In driving it is absolutely necessary to shoot high
and quickly, so as to avoid dropping the muzzle of the gun and
shooting underneath, particularly at grouse on the level or underneath you. There is little to guide the eye, and one has to rely
on calculation, which must be instantaneous, as to where to aim
that the spot in the air fired at will intercept the swift flight
of the bird. There are easy shots presenting themselves in every
drive ; ones that cannot well be missed, even by the beginner in

GROUSE. 77

driving, but with them come the most difficult that could possibly be imagined in game shooting, chances that practice alone can ensure being taken with invariable success. Driving is undoubtedly increasing in popularity with grouse shooters generally, and rivals walking in the shooting of grouse even in Scotland. Each mode of grouse shooting has its supporters, and even its devotees, and as each yields a large measure of sporting pleasure, it is unnecessary to compare the attractions or merits of driving on English moors as compared with the shooting over dogs on the rougher stretches of heather in the Highlands of Scotland.

PARTRIDGE SHOOTING.

OF the different game birds to be met with in this country, possibly none affords more enjoyment to the shooter than the partridge. More especially is this so in the case of that largely - represented class of shooting men— the possessors of only moderate means.

Partridge shooting, of course, can be, and is, carried out on a large and exten-

THE LITTLE BROWN BIRD.

sive scale in certain parts of the country, where everything is done to secure the production of a head of game as great as the acreage can possibly carry, and where neither time, money, nor expense are spared to fulfil this object. But whether the sportsman be rich or poor, a certain amount of partridge shooting is always within his reach, and, in the opinion of many, a far greater amount of enjoyable sport is to be obtained for a given sum of money with the "little brown bird" than with his more aristocratic rival— the pheasant.

It is not proposed to give here an exhaustive treatise upon the partridge, but it is hoped that this brief collection of notes and

PARTRIDGE. 79

suggestions may be of interest, and possibly of some service to the reader who is able to devote a short space of time to its perusal.

The prosperous condition of the country at the present time doubtless accounts for the great increase in the popularity of game shooting. The improved facilities of travelling enable busy men nowadays to put in a day's shooting occasionally at such a distance from home as would never have been dreamed of a few years ago.

It is fortunate that the partridge possesses a remarkable ability for adapting himself to surrounding circumstances. An ever-increasing population has necessitated encroachment upon many acres of land that once afforded good feeding ground and cover alike to the partridge, districts that once consisted of stretches of undulating cornfields and grassy meadows, with only an isolated dwelling dotted about here and there upon the landscape, long since having been converted into busy towns, bristling with human habitations and boasting of population of tens of thousands. But the partridge, however loth he may be to be driven from his favourite haunts, still thrives, and may be found to-day on the very outskirts of large manufacturing towns; and even within a very few miles of St. Paul's itself the discovery of a nest or a covey of birds is by no means so uncommon an event at the present time as might naturally be supposed.

The hen partridge, unlike the pheasant, is a most excellent mother. She displays, both as regards the position selected for her nest and the careful manner in which she will do all in her power to conceal her eggs from the observation of all possible enemies, an amount of caution which is indeed praiseworthy. And when the young are hatched the safety of their brood is the first consideration of the parent birds. How often have persons, ignorant of their habits, and coming suddenly upon a pair of partridges with their newly-hatched offspring, been deceived by the strange antics of the old birds? Fluttering along as if wounded and unable to rise more than a few inches from the ground, they will attract the attention of the passer-by until their young ones have reached a place of safety, when suddenly they will rise and fly away a couple of fields or more, leaving the astounded observer in a state of utter bewilderment at their marvellous powers of deception. But no sooner is the danger passed than they are back again, calling to their frightened

80 SHOOTING.

chicks, and bidding them leave their place of retreat—an invitation which meets with a ready response on the part of the scattered youngsters.

THE PARTRIDGE AND THE PLOUGH.

The draining and cultivation of waste land have done much to render suitable a considerable acreage of ground hitherto lacking in the requirements of the partridge. It has been asserted, with much truth, that the partridge follows the plough, and it is very evident that in the best cultivated districts, and notably where a large head of sheep is kept and a quantity of corn grown, the partridge thrives amazingly. So, too, in those parts where large tracts of land are being continually laid down to grass and kept principally for grazing purposes, the stock of partridges gradually diminishes, for not only is the supply of food in such places insufficient, but cover also, which partridges must have, is to a great extent wanting. Much can be done, however, in even such unpromising country as this, if good, thick hedges are preserved and patches of gorse, heather, and bracken are encouraged here and there. In addition to this, an artificial supply of food in some form or another— a few sheaves of corn, or some beans or peas scattered about from time to time in secluded places—should be forthcoming.

WATER.

The question of water supply is also an important one, and one too often overlooked by owners of shootings. If there is no natural supply of any sort, time will be well spent in supplying water in shady places for the birds to drink during the hot months of the year or when the rainfall is deficient. It is a well-known fact that on hot afternoons in September birds will often be found in considerable numbers in the vicinity of a stream or pool where they have congregated together for the purpose of drinking, and this, in itself, should be sufficient proof of the necessity of supplying water to the birds to drink where no natural supply is available. Food and drink are to be regarded as the two prime factors where animal life is concerned, but there are many other matters which

EARLY MORNING.

PARTRIDGE. 83

must not be disregarded by the man who would wish to have a goo l show of game.

There are, unfortunately, on many shooting properties certain causes that exist and which cannot be removed which render to a certain degree the preservation of game a difficult matter.

RIGHTS OF WAY.

Footpaths and rights of way across a shooting are amongst the worst of these, and a sharp look-out must be kept for suspicious-looking persons using them. The felling of timber, too, in the spring, at the very time when birds are choosing sites for their nests and commencing to lay, causes a serious disturbance in wooded districts, though this will affect partridges somewhat less than pheasants, except in cases in which the men, in going backwards and forwards to their work, have to traverse fields and hedges. It is sometimes difficult to deal with these men, who, as often as not, are complete strangers to the neighbourhood, and also, therefore, unlike the labourers employed upon the farm, have no actual interest in the welfare of the estate. The most that can be done is to go down and have a friendly chat with them, if such a thing is possible, or send the keeper down to see them, and ask them civilly to keep to the footpath as much as possible when going to or returning from work, and not to make any unnecessary noise. This, accompanied by a small donation towards the purchase of " refreshment," will probably have the desired effect. It is essential that the shooting tenant should be the best of friends with all those connected in any way, either directly or indirectly, with his shooting. Labourers on the farm will occasionally come across a nest in a dangerous place, or will " cut out " a nest in the hayfield, and the keeper should be empowered to give them a small reward upon the nest being pointed out to him. It is a great mistake to give rewards for eggs brought to the keeper's cottage, as such a proceeding is liable to lead to " egg-hunting " upon one's own land or upon the property of one's neighbour. Even in cases where immediate danger threatens the destruction of the eggs and necessitates their instant removal, the

G 2

84

SHOOTING.

nest should also be shown to the keeper, who will know at once whether it be a real or a fictitious one.

THE FARMER OF THE LAND.

The farmer or occupier of the land must not be forgotten either, but in his case a present of game every time the ground is shot over is the best means of enlisting his sympathies, and he will do his best to keep poachers off the ground.

VERMIN.

One of the most important duties of a keeper is the keeping in check of all kinds of vermin. Jays, magpies, and other egg-eating birds should be systematically kept down, as also must be weasels, stoats, rats, and hedgehogs. Then there will be always a prowling cat or a poaching dog to be reckoned with, either of which will probably do more harm in a short space of time, and particularly in the nesting season, than all the different kinds of vermin put together will do in a year. A bird on her nest suddenly startled, and perhaps nearly pounced upon by cat or dog, will seldom return, and a whole clutch of eggs is thereby lost. In the case of cats the keeper will know how to deal with them, and a wandering dog is generally identified without much difficulty, when a firm but polite request should at once be made to his owner to keep him at home. If the offence is repeated, the threat of a claim for damages will be better than the destruction of a dog that may be of value to his master, and it should be remembered that to kill a domestic animal is an offence against the law which may involve the perpetrator or his master in a heavy payment for damages to the owner of the animal.

It is much to be regretted that owls and kestrels are so ruthlessly destroyed by many keepers. That occasional individuals of the hawk tribe will take to game-destroying is not to be denied, but as these birds are all most valuable to the game preserver and the farmer as the destroyers of vermin, only those that are actually caught red-handed should be shot. The balance of good done by owls of all sorts is so greatly in excess of any damage committed by them that an owner of a shooting should, so far from

PARTRIDGE. 85

permitting them to be destroyed, absolutely forbid his keeper to molest them. At the most the only sin that can be laid to their charge is the occasional capture of a young rabbit, and no man should grudge them that much in return for the great amount of benefit they bestow upon the game preserver in the killing of rats, which are to be reckoned amongst the worst destroyers of eggs and young birds.

As compared with the number of pheasants reared annually in this country, comparatively few partridges are brought up by hand, and on the majority of shootings only those eggs which are picked up from nests in dangerous places are put under hens by the keeper. Even in this case, unless a fair quantity are brought in at a time, it is hardly worth while to go to the trouble of placing the eggs under hens with all the consequent worry and bother of bringing up the young birds to follow. Far better is it when only a few eggs come to hand at one time to distribute them amongst other nests known to the keeper, but care must be taken not to put eggs already half incubated into a nest where the bird has only just begun to sit, or vice versa, for the partridge, as soon as the eggs in the more advanced stage are hatched off, will go off with the young ones and the remaining eggs will be left to perish. In cases of doubt as to whether the picked-up eggs are fresh or partially incubated, and when no means of testing them are ready to hand, they should be given to a hen. Even then, when on the point of hatching, they may be put into the nests of any birds whose eggs have arrived at the same stage of incubation, and unless she has already got a full clutch of eggs on the point of hatching, the hen partridge will be quite capable of rearing three or four extra chicks besides her own.

An excellent plan, lately recommended by a writer to the "Field," whereby the possible theft of eggs from any nest may be to a great extent avoided, is to have at hand several "dummy," or imitation, partridge eggs, and when a nest in a dangerous situation is discovered, the sham eggs, which should have a small mark for identification on the under side, may be substituted for the real ones, the latter being put under a hen until "chipped," when they may be put back again into the nest, and the dummy eggs removed. Great care must, however, be exercised in the carrying out of this

86   SHOOTING.

operation, and the sitting bird must on no account be disturbed, the act of taking away or replacing the eggs being performed while she is off the nest at feeding time, when the keeper can approach the nest and change the eggs unobserved. This plan serves the double purpose of reducing the risks of the real eggs being stolen to a minimum, and, in the event of the eggs being taken, of enabling their identification should the poacher be apprehended with the eggs upon him, for in his hurry he will not stay to closely examine them when he removes the eggs from the nest to his pocket. If, however, he gets away without being detected, and discovers subsequently that he has been taken in, he will not care ever to risk again the chance of being caught in trying to steal eggs which, after all, may be worthless to him.

Much more could be written, did space permit it, upon the various points to be observed in order to obtain the greatest amount of success in the preservation of partridges, but, in addition to the foregoing remarks, it will be sufficient here to remind the shooting owner that everything depends upon the vigilance of his keeper, not only during the nesting season, but throughout the entire year. On those estates where no artificial rearing of partridges is attempted, the keeper will be able to give the greater part of his time and attention to the warding off of any evils which from time to time may arise, and to the improvement of natural conditions, together with the making good of deficiencies wherever possible.

A GOOD KEEPER.

And now we may pass on to discuss the subject from another point of view—the shooting side of the question. Here, too, the keeper has many important duties to perform, and the organisation of a day's shooting will be probably better carried out if he is left to do it in his own way, for this is certainly a part of his business. Moreover, it is to his interest to show as much sport as possible to his master's guests, and he is, if he has any pretension to being a capable man, better able, from his knowledge of the habits of birds and of his beat, to conduct affairs to the best possible advantage.

Partridge shooting in this country is conducted in three different ways; walking up early in the season in whatever cover is available,

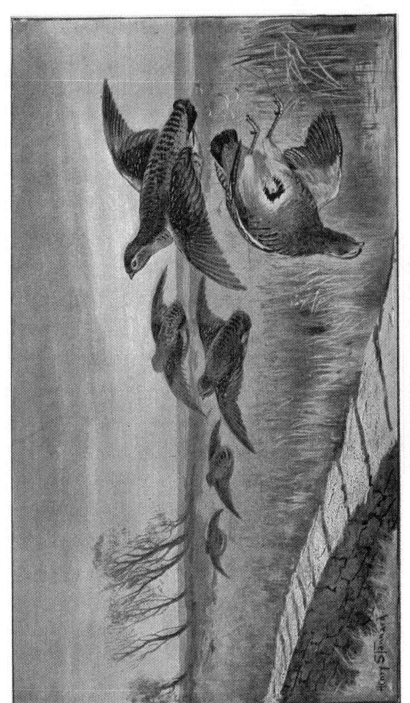

THEIR NUMBER REDUCED BY ONE.

PARTRIDGE. 89

driving with the aid of beaters, and, lastly, walking up under the kite. The first is, doubtless, when birds are not too wild and there is a fair amount of cover to hold them, a most enjoyable form of sport, but it is not always by any means satisfactory.

SHOTS OUT OF RANGE.

Too often, when cover is deficient and birds are consequently difficult to approach, there is a tendency to take long shots at birds which are really beyond sporting range, with the result that a large number of birds are "pricked," or slightly wounded, without being brought to bag, and for this reason the habit is strongly to be deprecated.

WALKING UP.

The amount of pleasure to be derived from walking up partridges in September or early in October, when the sportsman is young and active, birds plentiful and cover good, is very great, and under these circumstances a more enjoyable occupation cannot be imagined; but it must be remembered that experience has proved that, if this practice is pursued too persistently, it will be at the expense of the value of the shooting in after years. After a day's walking up birds, it will generally be found that a very large proportion of the bag consists of young birds of the year, and this, after a successful breeding season, is only natural; but it should be the aim and the object of every true sportsman to kill off the older birds as much as possible, and not thin the young birds too severely.

DRIVING.

This result is best obtained by driving, and, for this reason partly, driving has increased in popularity of recent years to a very great extent, the pity being that many parts of the country are quite unsuitable for it. When birds are driven, the old ones, for the most part, come first and occupy the shooter's attention, and many there are who, when once they have acquired a certain amount of skill in bringing down birds driven over them at a high rate of speed, are ready to declare that no finer sport exists, and that the killing of a brace of driven birds with a quick right and left gives more pleasure and satisfaction

BACK COME SOME BIRDS.

than the bagging of half-a-dozen birds walked up in a field of turnips. Driving, too, gives a far greater variety of shots and many more

PARTRIDGE. 91

difficult ones than is the case when birds are walked up in cover, and sport can often be provided for a greater number of guns when birds are driven, owing to the fact that the birds present an extended front to the guns, thereby affording a much greater number of shots than when they rise in a mass.

CONSIDERABLE PRACTICE.

Considerable practice will be necessary before the shooter can become even a moderate shot at driven birds, and in the difficulty of the performance lies its greatest charm. Many men have become disheartened because they have been out for a whole week, perhaps, shooting at driven birds, and have scarcely touched a feather, but this has been the experience of most men when they first took up this form of shooting, although they have been able to hold their own previously in good company at other kinds of shooting.

A well-fitting gun is a sine qua non when quick shooting is a necessity, as in driving, for with birds coming at lightning speed there is no time to dwell upon your bird or correct your aim. It goes without saying, too, that your ammunition must be of the very best, a too common cause of failure in shooting being the use of inferior and badly-loaded cartridges, lacking in velocity and penetration. Every shooting man, whether he possesses a shooting of his own or not, is glad to get invitations from his friends to join them in a day's sport, but it must be remembered that few men care to turn their shooting ground into a practice ground for beginners.

MANY INVITATIONS.

The man who is a good performer will get many invitations from friends, but the poor shot will seldom be asked out, and he will not much enjoy his day when he does receive an invitation if he is the duffer of the party. Hence it follows that the man who would shoot really well must, even if equipped with the most perfect gun and the best of cartridges, have sufficient practice to keep his eye in—in season and out—and whether he has a shooting of his own or not he will find that a few afternoons at intervals throughout the year spent in practice at clay birds, thrown at all sorts of angles and different elevations, will not have been spent in vain.

PHEASANT SHOOTING.

It is very satisfactory to note the steady increase in the number of shootings on which the rearing of pheasants by hand is indulged in to a greater or less extent. There can be little doubt that, if artificial breeding were abandoned altogether, there would very soon be no pheasants at all in many districts. The enormous increase in the number of game farms, where thousands of pheasants are brought up annually and from which a vast number of eggs are sent to all parts of the kingdom, is sufficient and striking evidence of the attention that is paid to pheasant shooting at the present time.

LAYING IN CAPTIVITY.

It is indeed fortunate that the pheasant lays so well in captivity, as thereby the labour of collecting the eggs of the wild bird is entirely done away with, and a quantity of eggs are available at one time for placing under hens.

The wild pheasant is not so successful in family matters as could be wished, and it is a sad, but, at the same time, a much too common sight to come across wild broods of two or three, or perhaps of a single chick—if the term " brood " can be applied to one solitary individual.

Some hen pheasants do, of course, make fairly good mothers, and in this respect the old-fashioned, dark-necked variety (Phasianus Colchicus) is considered by many to be superior to other birds. Untunately, this variety appears to have died out in many parts, having been superseded by the ring-necked bird of Chinese origin. However, of late years a reaction appears to have set in, and a fresh demand for the dark-necked variety has arisen, so that it is to be hoped that these exceedingly handsome birds will shortly be-

THROUGH THE BRACKEN.

PHEASANT. 95

come more common. Certain it is that both P. Colchicus and P. Torquatus are first-rate sporting birds, but, as one kind will occasionally thrive better than the other in a particular district, it is as well, perhaps, to give both a trial, selecting finally the one that appears to succeed best in the locality.

The popularity of the pheasant as a game bird has placed within the reach of the poorest classes an article of food at a reasonable price, and highly esteemed by the many. In November and December, when the " big shoots " take place, thousands of these birds find their way into the markets, good specimens being procurable at an absurdly low price. It has often been remarked that pheasant shooting is a sport only for the rich; but this is not necessarily the case by any means. Someone rather cleverly remarked a long time ago that when one went covert shooting and a pheasant rose, it was a case of "up gets a sovereign, bang goes twopence, and down comes half-a-crown." How gladly nowadays would those who market a portion of their birds take two-and-sixpence apiece all round for them. But if one cannot make sure of this price in these days, it can at least be urged that the cost of production and the price of cartridges are proportionately lower.

COST OF PHEASANT REARING.

Considerable discussion arises in the sporting papers annually as to the cost of pheasant rearing, and many and varied estimates have been given, some having placed the cost as low as three shillings per head, while others contend that their birds cost them five times that amount. So much depends upon the weather, the locality, the price of feeding-stuffs, and the competence of one's keeper, that it is impossible to lay down a hard and fast rule as to the probable expense that will be incurred ere the birds are brought to the gun.

It may, perhaps, be as well to mention here that it will be very much to the advantage of the owner of a shooting to acquaint himself as far as possible with certain important subjects connected with pheasant rearing, as by so doing he will be able in a great measure to check waste and extravagance.

No wise man will engage a keeper without having previously

96   SHOOTING.

made the strictest enquiry as to his character, and satisfied himself
that the man he proposes to employ is thoroughly competent to
perform the duties expected of him.

It is not to be expected that any owner of a shooting will be
able to supervise personally the purchasing of food, etc., but accounts
should always be kept.

THE HEAD OF GAME.

As regards the necessary annual supply of pheasant eggs to be
placed under hens for hatching, it rests entirely with the proprietor of
a shooting estate whether he will pen a number of birds on his own
place to produce these eggs or whether he will purchase the eggs
direct from one of the many pheasant farms now in existence. The
former plan has a great deal to recommend it, as by its adoption
the keeper is made responsible, to a great extent, for the good
quality of the eggs produced. When eggs are purchased from any
game farmers who have a reputation to lose, freshness and fertility
being guaranteed by the respective vendors, no attention should be
paid to grumblings on the score of infertility, unless the so-called
stale or unfertile eggs are forthcoming in order that a searching examination into the circumstances of the case may be made.

MOVABLE PENS.

Of recent years the practice of keeping the laying birds in
movable pens has become very popular, and there is no doubt that
the adoption of the system has been attended with very marked
success; but the pens should be as large as is compatible with their
easy removal. This operation is best carried out by the employment of a couple of pens to each lot of birds, not more than five
or six hens being allowed to each cock. The pens should be placed
close together, side by side, and should have large sliding doors
on either side, so that when it is wished to remove the birds from
one pen to the other, it is simply necessary to pull open by the
aid of a cord fixed to each of them the adjacent doors in either pen.
This done, the birds will, generally of their own accord, find their way
into their new quarters in a few minutes, when the door of the

ROCKETTING PHEASANTS.

PHEASANT. 99

fresh pen may be closed by pulling the cord fixed to the opposite end, the pen that the birds have just left being brought over and placed on the opposite side of the one into which the birds have just entered, where it will be in position for the repetition of the operation, which should be carried out at least two or three times a week. Of course, it is immaterial whether the doors are placed at the ends or sides of the pens, but in the latter case it will be longer before the end of the field is reached, which is an advantage. By the adoption of this principle the birds will be always upon fresh ground, and the moving process will be carried out with little disturbance to the occupants of the pens—a matter of very great importance where birds naturally so shy have to be dealt with. Hinged doors also, at the top of each pen at either end, will be required to facilitate the removal of the eggs—which should be collected once a day at the time of the evening meal, but one or two "nest eggs" should always be kept at each corner of the pen, underneath the pieces of brushwood placed there to gratify the hen's desire for concealment whilst laying. The same person should always be employed to collect the eggs, feed the birds, and move the pens, and strangers on no account should be permitted to come near the penned birds. The further precaution also should be taken of having the tops of the pens made of string-netting instead of wire, even though it may have to be renewed periodically, so that in the case of any possible alarm the birds may not injure themselves by flying upwards. Small-meshed wire netting should be employed for the sides, small enough to keep out rats or other vermin, and the pens should stand quite evenly on the ground, any depressions under the sides being filled up with sods of turf. A ditch to carry off water in the case of a heavy thunderstorm must be cut round the pens to prevent flooding, and ample shelter should be provided for the birds by placing some old sacks or thick fir boughs upon the tops of the enclosures.

Considerable difficulty is often experienced in obtaining a sufficient number of broody hens to take the eggs as they are laid, and the keeper should therefore make arrangements beforehand with the farmers and cottagers of the district to take all the hens that they can spare during the spring as they become broody. At the same

н 2

time, an incubator will be of great assistance if started simultaneously with the setting of, say, ten or a dozen hens, as by that means, in the case of the partial failure of any brood, it may be made up to its proper number with chicks from the incubator. So much has been written on the rearing of pheasants and the facilities for so doing, especially in the matter of foods, which have been so greatly increased in recent years, that it will be sufficient here to draw attention to one or two points of special importance.

THE REARING OF YOUR BIRDS.

Where all live creatures in a domesticated state are concerned, it is advisable that the ordinary conditions under which those creatures are wont to exist in a state of Nature should be as nearly fulfilled as possible. Young pheasants in a wild state subsist very largely upon ants' eggs, and these should be provided whenever they are to be obtained. With reference also to the much-discussed question as to the advisability or otherwise of providing the young birds with a supply of water to drink, many keepers declare that they are strongly in favour of the practice, while there are others who assert that they have achieved the greatest amount of success with exactly the opposite treatment. It seems only natural, however,

PHEASANT. 101

that birds should do better with than without a supply of water, and, in any case, it can do them no harm. If water is offered to them they will drink it readily, and it is more than likely that its use is denounced by some for the very good or either bad reason that the giving of it entails a good deal of extra trouble.

The provision of shelter in the form of boughs of evergreen, under which the little birds can run when alarmed, and which will serve as a protection from the sun, rain, and wind, is very necessary.

The same remarks that have been made in the chapter on the partridge as to the destruction of vermin will apply here also, and special attention will have to be directed to this matter as soon as the young pheasants are turned into the woods. It is a little mortifying for a keeper to find one morning on going his rounds that a fox has levied toll to the extent of perhaps twenty or thirty of his birds during the night, and, unless he is himself a keen huntsman, as many keepers are, it is more than likely that that fox will come to an untimely end.

IN HUNTING LOCALITIES.

In a hunting locality, however, the shooting man, even though his sporting proclivities lie in other directions, should be careful to do nothing which may interfere in the slightest degree with that feeling of good-fellowship which should exist between all sportsmen.

THE OLD STYLE OF SHOOTING.

The shooting of pheasants is carried on nowadays in a manner very different to that pursued by our forefathers. In the olden days sportsmen (and sportsmen they certainly were) derived much pleasure from seeing their dogs work and in getting a shot now and again at a bird as he rose from the tangled undergrowth, but, although it is certain that the keen shooting man of the present time is in every way entitled to be called a sportsman just as much as was his grandfather, the old style of shooting has, to a great extent, in the natural

102 SHOOTING.

order of things, owing to causes which cannot be enumerated here, given place to a new form altogether. The chief reason for this may be that many sportsmen, who are for the most part busy men, expect nowadays to kill fifty brace of birds in a day, while formerly they would have been content to have spread that amount of shooting over a whole week; but, whatever the cause, pheasant shooting with the aid of beaters is to-day more extensively indulged in than ever, and it is the only method by which a fair head of game may be bagged in a limited space of time.

Early in the season, while the hedgerows are still in leaf, and the coverts are not ready to shoot, many an enjoyable day may be spent in trying the hedgerows and patches of brakes and gorse with a spaniel or two for a few outlying birds, and there are few men who will not gladly take such an opportunity when it offers.

A FINE OCTOBER DAY.

Nothing can be more delightful on a fine October day than to bag five or ten brace of birds under such conditions, and what man is there who, having been kept for several days in London, does not appreciate the glories of the countryside and mark the beauties of the woods, tinged here and there with those lovely shades of brown and yellow that herald the approach of autumn?

But it is when the time arrives for the coverts to be shot, which will not be until the trees have shed the greater portion of their leaves, that the skill of the shooter will be tested to its fullest extent. When birds are plentiful and the keeper knows how to organise his beaters, what splendid chances of really sporting shots he can provide for his master's guests!

Gradually, beat by beat, the birds will be driven from one piece of coppice to another, but in all cases, so far as the nature of the ground will permit, so as to present the tallest and most difficult of sporting shots as they come over the guns.

This is the essence of true sport, and the man who can succeed in bringing down a dozen rocketters in succession at the last stand of the day will assuredly go home well pleased with his day's sport and his own performance.

PIGEON SHOOTING.

THE type of gun suitable for shooting live pigeons from traps differs very considerably from the game gun. A heavy charge of

THE "GRAND PRIX" PIGEON GUN.

powder and shot are employed, hence a heavy gun; besides, weight steadies the muscles and absorbs recoil. Such a gun, for in-

104 SHOOTING.

stance, would scale about 7½lb., being chambered for the 12-bore cartridge, 2¾in. in length, and should shoot 1¼oz. of shot with a high velocity, namely, great penetration force.

PENETRATION.

Too much stress cannot be laid upon this point, as so often do pigeon shooters talk of what such and such a gun will do in pattern, but omit altogether what such and such a gun will do when combined with velocity; for it is far better to have fewer pellets penetrate well than have a bird " dusted " with a multitude.

PATTERN.

For the short distance man the right barrel should be not quite full choke, but otherwise that barrel as well as the left should be full choke.

An easy alignment of the gun is best attained with a deadened top rib, broad at the breech and narrowing towards the muzzle, whilst a half-pistol grip stock is generally preferred by the most successful votaries.

Guns with single trigger, in opposition to those with double triggers, although so recently introduced, are now used by some of the most successful shots of the day, one of the reasons no doubt being the quick and ready discharge of the second barrel without moving the hand to fire the second cartridge, and consequently the alignment is not altered, and the swing not arrested.

GOOD BALANCE.

An all-important matter in a pigeon gun is to have it not only well balanced, but the weight so distributed that the gun handles freely and comes up quickly on the object without any effort, notwithstanding its 7½lb. weight.

In some pigeon shooting clubs the maximum weight of the gun is 7½lb., and the charge of shot 1¼oz.

THE BLUE-ROCK PIGEON—MALE AND FEMALE.

PIGEON. 107

PIGEON SHOOTING RULES.

(Published by "THE FIELD.")

HURLINGHAM CLUB RULES.

Revised May, 1898.

1. The Referee's decision shall be final.

2. A miss-fire is no shot, provided the shooter has a cap on the gun, and if it be cocked and loaded, or, in the case of a breech-loader, if the cartridge does not explode.

3. If the shooter's gun miss-fire with the first barrel and he use the second and miss, the bird is to be scored lost.

4. If the miss-fire occurs with the second barrel, the shooter having failed to kill with his first, he may claim another bird; but he must fire off the first barrel with a cap on, and a full charge of powder, or, in the case of a breech-loader, with a blank cartridge, before firing the second. And he must not pull both triggers at the same time.

5. The shooter in a match or sweepstakes shall be at his shooting mark at the expiration of two minutes from the last shot, unless in the case of an accident, when the Referee shall decide what time shall be allowed to remedy the accident.

6. The shooter's feet shall be behind the shooting mark until after his gun is discharged. If, in the opinion of the Referee, the shooter is baulked by any antagonist or looker on, or by the trapper, whether by accident or otherwise, he may be allowed another bird.

7. The shooter, when he is at his mark ready to shoot, shall give the caution, "Are you ready?" to the puller, and then call "Pull." Should the trap be pulled without the word being given, the shooter may take the bird or not; but if he fires, the bird must be deemed to be taken.

8. If, on the trap being pulled, the bird does not rise, it is at the option of the shooter to take it or not; if not, he must declare it by saying "No bird"; but should he fire after declaring, it is not to be scored for or against him.

9. If a bird that has been shot at perches or settles on the top of the fence or on any part of the buildings higher than the fence, it is to be scored a lost bird, unless it can be gathered by the man without using any appliance or getting off the ground.

10. If a bird once out of the ground should return and fall dead within the boundary, it must be scored a lost bird.

11. If the shooter advances to the mark and orders the trap to be pulled, and does not shoot at the bird, or his gun is not properly loaded, or does not go off, owing to his own negligence, that bird is to be scored lost.

SHOOTING.

12. Should a bird that has been shot at be flying away, and a by-stander fires and brings the bird down within the boundary, the Referee may, if satisfied the bird would not have fallen by the gun of the shooter, order it to be scored a lost bird; or, if satisfied that the bird would have fallen, may order it to be scored a dead bird; or, if in doubt on the subject, he may order the shooter to shoot at another bird.

13. A bird shot on the ground with the first barrel is "No bird," but it may be shot on the ground with the second barrel, if it has been fired at with the first barrel while on the wing; but if the shooter misses with the first and discharges his second barrel, it is to be accounted a lost bird, in case of not falling within bounds.

14. Only one person to be allowed to pick up the bird (or a dog, if the shooter will allow it). No instrument is to be used for this purpose. All birds must be gathered by the dog or trapper, and no member shall have the right to gather his own bird, or to touch it with his hand or gun.

15. In Single Shooting, if more than one bird is liberated, the shooter may call "No bird," and claim another shot; but if he shoots he must abide by the consequences.

16. The shooter must not leave the shooting mark under any pretence to follow up any bird that will not rise, nor may he return to his mark after he has once quitted it to fire his second barrel.

17. In matches or in sweepstakes when shot is limited, any shooter found to have in his gun more shot than is allowed is to be at once disqualified.

18. Any shooter is compelled to unload his gun on being challenged; but if the charge is found not to exceed the allowance, the challenger shall pay forthwith £1 to the shooter.

19. None but members can shoot except on the occasion of private matches.

20. No wire cartridges or concentrators allowed, or other substance to be mixed with the shot.

21. In all handicaps, sweepstakes, or matches, the standard bore of the gun is No. 12. Members shooting with less to go in at the rate of half a yard for every bore less than 12 down to 16-bore. Eleven-bore guns to stand back half a yard from the handicap distance, and no guns over 11-bore allowed.

22. The winner of a sweepstakes of the value of ten sovereigns, including his own stake, goes back two yards; under that sum, one yard, provided there be over five shooters. Members saving or dividing in an advertised event will be handicapped accordingly.

23. Should any member shoot at a distance nearer than that at which he is handicapped, it shall be scored no bird.

24. That for the future the charge of powder is limited to four drachms. Chilled shot and "sawdust" powder may be used. The

PIGEON. 109

weight of guns not to exceed 7 lb. 8 oz. Size of shot restricted to Nos. 5, 6, 7, and 8. Charge of shot limited to 1¼ oz.

25. All muzzle-loaders shall be loaded with shot from the Club bowls.

26. If any bird escapes through any opening in the paling, it shall be a "No bird," if in the Referee's opinion it could not have flown over the palings, but in no instance shall it be scored a dead bird.

27. From the 1st of May the advertised events shall begin at three o'clock, unless otherwise notified, and no shooter will be admitted after the end of the second round in any advertised event.

28. No scouting allowed on the Club premises, and no pigeon to be shot at in the shooting ground except by the shooter standing at his mark. Anyone infringing this rule will be fined £1.

RULES FOR DOUBLE RISES.

1. In Double Shooting, when more than two traps are pulled, the shooter may call "No birds," and claim two more; but if he shoots, he must abide by the consequences.

2. If, on the traps being pulled, the birds do not rise, it is at the option of the shooter to take them or not. If not, he must declare by saying "No birds."

3. If, on the traps being pulled, one bird does not rise, he cannot demand another double rise; but he must wait and take the bird when it flies.

4. A bird shot on the ground, if the other bird is missed, is a lost bird; but if the other bird is killed, the shooter may demand another two birds.

5. If the shooter's gun misses fire with the first barrel, he may demand another two birds; but if he fires his second barrel he must abide by the consequences. If the miss-fire occurs with the second barrel, the shooter having killed with the first, he may demand another bird, but may only use one barrel; if he missed with his first barrel, Rule 5 in Single Shooting will apply.

A bird falling dead on the Scoring Box is to be counted for the shooter.

GUN CLUB RULES.
Revised May, 1898.

1. A miss-fire with first barrel is no shot under any circumstances. If the shooter miss fire with the second barrel he shall have another shot, but with the ordinary charge of powder and no shot in the first barrel.

2. If the gun be locked, or not cocked, or not loaded, and the bird flies away, it is a "lost bird;" if the stock or cock should break in the act of firing it is "no bird."

110 SHOOTING.

3. If the trap is pulled without notice from the shooter, he has the option to take the bird or not.

4. The puller shall not pull the trap until the trapper and the dog are back in their places, even should the shooter call "Pull."

5. If, on the trap being pulled, the bird does not rise, the shooter to take it or not at his option; but if not, he must declare it by saying "No bird" before it is on the wing. If, however, the bird rises and settles before the shooter fires, it shall be at his option to refuse it or not.

6. If more than one bird be liberated, the shooter has the option of calling "No bird."

7. In shooting at a bird, should both barrels go off at once it shall score the same as if they had been let off "separately."

8. A bird to be scored good must be gathered by the dog or man without the aid of a ladder or any other instrument, and all birds not gathered in the ground, or gathered inside the pavilion enclosure, having flown over the railings, to be scored lost.

9. If a bird which has been shot perches or settles on the top of the fence, or on any of the buildings in the ground higher than the fence, it is to be scored a "lost bird."

10. If a bird once out of the ground return and fall dead within the boundary, it must be scored a "lost bird."

11. If the first barrel be fired whilst the bird is on the ground, should the bird be killed by either barrel it is "no bird;" if missed, it is lost. It may be shot on the ground with the second barrel, if it has been fired at with the first barrel while on the wing.

12. The shooter is bound at once to gather his bird, or depute some person so to do when called upon; but in so doing he must not be assisted by any other person, or use any description of implement. Should the shooter be in any way baffled by his opponent, or by any other person or dog, he can claim another bird with the sanction of the Referee.

13. The shooter having once left the mark after shooting at the bird, cannot shoot at it again under any circumstances.

14. In matches or in sweepstakes, any shooter found to have in his gun any more shot or powder than is allowed, to be at once disqualified.

15. Any shooter is compelled to unload his gun on being challenged; but if the charge is found not to exceed the allowance, the challenger shall pay £1 to the shooter, which must be paid before he (the challenger) shoots again.

16. Officers of the Army and Navy on full pay, provided they are bona fide guests of a member for the day, are allowed to shoot in any sweepstakes to which the Club does not add prize or money. Members accredited from recognised Foreign Clubs shall only be

PIGEON.

111

allowed to shoot for four weeks during the season, after which they must be proposed and seconded as candidates if they desire to shoot.

17. Breech-loaders not to be loaded until the shooter is at the mark, and the trapper has returned to his place. On leaving the mark, should a cartridge not have been discharged, it is to be removed before the shooter turns his face from the traps.

18. No wire cartridges allowed; nor is any bone dust or other substance to be mixed with the shot.

19. Should any shooter shoot at a distance nearer than his proper distance, the bird, if killed, is "no bird;" if missed, a "lost bird;" but should he, by direction of the Referee or Scorer, shoot at any wrong distance, the bird, if missed, shall be "no bird," and the shooter shall be allowed another, which, if killed, shall be scored.

20. 1¼oz. of shot and 4dr. of black powder, or its equivalent in any other description of gunpowder, is the maximum charge.

21. In shooting for the principal advertised events members can enter before the commencement of the third round, unless it shall be within the knowledge of the Referee that any member proposing to enter has been on the ground during the first round, in which case he shall not be permitted to shoot after the commencement of the second round; for all other sweepstakes, entries must be made before the commencement of the second round.

22. The sweepstakes preceding the chief event of the day shall be divided in equal proportions by those shooters who may be in at the end of the round at or after three o'clock, as the Referee may direct.

23. The baskets containing the birds for the whole day's shooting shall be numbered by paint at the back. The baskets, in the order they are to be brought out and trapped, shall be drawn for by the Referee, and the baskets so marked shall be used in the order of rotation in which they are drawn.

HANDICAPPING RULES.

24. That a Handicapper who does not shoot or bet on pigeon shooting be appointed by the Club.

25. That a new handicap be made previous to the commencement of each shooting season.

26. That when the handicap is made the distances shall range from twenty-two to thirty-three yards.

27. That three members of the Club be appointed as a Shooting Committee, to whom the Handicapper shall submit his new handicap for approval at the commencement of each shooting season. This Committee to receive complaints of members about their handicap distances; two to form a quorum.

SHOOTING.

28. That during the season the Handicapper shall alter the handicap according to his judgment previous to each shooting day.

29. That every new member shall commence at twenty-six yards, except the Handicapper has special reasons to the contrary.

30. In handicap sweepstakes, winners of £5 go back one yard; £10 and upwards, two yards; £20 and over, three yards for the day. These penalties do not apply to the advertised events of the day unless they have been incurred in such advertised events.

31. In handicaps the amount of division is to be declared to the Referee, and the members dividing shall be penalised to the amount they receive. This Rule not to apply to the saving of stakes. All penalties for winning to be exclusive of the winner's stake.

---

32. In large sweepstakes, if the money be over £50, there shall be two prizes; if over £100, three prizes; and over £200, four prizes.

33. No shooting at birds thrown up or other irregular practice with guns shall be permitted on the ground at any time.

34. Should two members agree to save stakes, and one of these divide with a third person, the member so dividing shall pay the full stake to the member who does not win or divide.

35. No member to be allowed to shoot in any sweepstakes or handicap until he shall have paid the amount of his entry to the Scorer, and should he shoot without having paid his stake before firing his first shot, he may be excluded from taking further part in such competition.

36. Saving of stakes shall apply to any member winning or dividing the first, second, third, or fourth prize, unless otherwise mutually agreed upon.

37. The deductions from all sweepstakes of the value of £8 and upwards in the summer season, and £5 and upwards in the winter season, is 10 per cent., to go to the funds of the Club.

38. No guns above 11-bore allowed.

39. Members shooting under an assumed name must have the same registered in a book by the Secretary. Only one assumed name is allowed, except by special sanction of the Committee.

The following fines will be strictly enforced:—

1. No bet shall be made by any member who has been called up to shoot after passing the enclosure gate, even should he have been standing there previous to his name being called. Any member infringing this rule will be fined £5, which shall be paid before he shoots again.

2. Pointing a gun at anyone, or firing a loaded gun without permission, except at the mark, £5.

3. Any person firing at a bird after it has passed the safety flags will be fined £5, and the bird shall be scored lost.

PIGEON. 113

RULES OF THE MEMBERS' £100 CHALLENGE CUP.

This Cup must be won three times consecutively to become the property of the winner. The minimum number of shooters is five, and the entry £5 each, but the Committee have the option of making the stakes £25 each when they consider it desirable. Distance thirty yards. Competitions for this Cup are continuous from year to year. The Cup not to be shot for before the first Saturday in May in each season.

RULES OF THE TUESDAY HANDICAP CUP, VALUE £50.

This Cup must be won twice consecutively, or four times in the season, to become the property of the winner. Ten per cent. is deducted every competition for the accumulative fund, until it be won. The minimum number of shooters is eight. Entry, £3.

GENERAL PIGEON SHOOTING RULES.

Enclosed grounds. The fence is the boundary, as at the Hurlingham Club and the Gun Club.

Open boundary, 80 yards from the centre trap where obtainable, or else the fence the boundary. A line to be run out level with the shooter who stands the farthest from the trap; and a bird falling dead behind this line cannot be scored. Traps five yards apart.

When a bird perches on a fence, tree, or building, and closes its wings, it is a lost bird. If it falls inside the boundary before closing its wings, it is scored to the shooter.

In the North the general rule is one trap, 21 yards rise. Gun to be held below the elbow until the bird is on the wing. 1oz. shot; boundary 60 yards.

In shooting from H and T traps both traps are to be filled; only one barrel allowed; distance from 21 to 35 yards. No spring traps permitted.

THE HURLINGHAM CLUB BOUNDARY.

The Hurlingham Club boundary is about 90 yards in a straight line from the centre trap.

THE GUN CLUB BOUNDARY.

The Gun Club (Notting Hill) boundary is 65 yards in a straight line from the centre trap.

THE MONACO BOUNDARY.

The Monaco boundary (a wire fence about 40 inches high) is 17 metres, or 18 yards 21¼ inches, in a straight line from the centre trap.

114   SHOOTING.

INANIMATE BIRD SHOOTING.

THE Ranelagh Club was the first place in England where this
kind of amusement or sport was indulged in; meetings were held
there in 1875.

The "Encyclopædia of Sport" states :—

> In 1887 Messrs. Cogswell and Harrison brought out the well-
> known Swiftsure trap and bird, and started the manufacture for the
> first time in England, substituting a pitch compound for the red
> clay that had hitherto been the material employed.

WHAT IS THE BIRD?

The bird is an inverted saucer thrown from a machine so that
the bird gyrates on its own axis, and so keeps "edge on" during
its flight.

EFFECT OF INANIMATE BIRD SHOOTING.

The effect of the introduction of this class of shooting greatly
facilitated the work of the shooting schools, as described by the
"Encyclopædia of Sport" as follows :—

> One of the most remarkable results attendant on the introduction
> of artificial target shooting has been the establishment of shooting
> schools, where the young gunner is quickly taught to handle his
> weapon in a workmanlike manner, and errors of fit are discovered
> and rectified by the try-gun and other means. It is now also ad-
> mitted by the most conservative sportsmen that clay bird shooting
> is excellent practice for field shooting generally, and that a season
> at clay birds will enable the average shot and novice to render a
> far better account of himself at "fur and feather" than would other-
> wise be the case. The same result would, of course, be obtained by
> pigeon shooting, but the cost is many times greater.

INANIMATE BIRDS. 115

OFFICIAL RULES

OF THE

INANIMATE BIRD SHOOTING ASSOCIATION.

GENERAL SHOOTING RULES.

ARRANGEMENT OF FIRING MARKS.

1. There shall be five firing marks, five yards apart, and shooters shall stand at not less than eighteen yards from the traps. The marks shall be numbered 1, 2, 3, 4, and 5, No. 1 being on the extreme left and No. 5 on the extreme right.

GUN AND AMMUNITION.

2. No gun of a larger calibre than 12-gauge shall be used, and the charge of shot shall not exceed 1⅛oz.

CHALLENGING GUNS, ETC.

3. The gun or cartridges of any shooter may be challenged by a competitor as not being in accordance with Rule 2, and, if found on examination to be a breach of the Rule, the holder of such gun or ammunition shall pay a fine of 10s. 6d. to the Club funds, and be disqualified from the current competition; but if the gun or ammunition be found correct, the challenger, except it be the Referee, shall pay 2s. 6d. to the Club funds.

UNAUTHORISED DISCHARGE OF GUN.

4. A shooter who, from any cause whatever, shall discharge his gun otherwise than in accordance with the regulations shall be excluded from taking part in any further competitions during the day. All firing at passing birds, animals, or other unauthorised objects shall be strictly prohibited.

DOUBLE DISCHARGE OF GUN.

5. If a shooter, in firing at a bird, shall let off both barrels practically at once, and kill his bird, that bird shall be scored a "no bird," and if he misses, the bird shall be scored a miss.

REFEREE.

6. A Referee shall be appointed to judge all matches, and his decision shall be final.

I 2

SHOOTING.

REFEREE'S DUTIES.

7. The Referee shall see that the traps are properly set, and he shall also see that all due precautions are taken by shooters for the safety of the trappers, shooters, and others.

PRECAUTIONS AGAINST ACCIDENTS.

8. All guns must be kept open at the breech while the traps are being re-filled, and until the trappers have returned to their places. Any person infringing this rule shall be fined one shilling. This rule does not apply to cases where there is a trench or other device enabling the traps to be re-filled while shooting is proceeding.

"NO BIRDS" FROM FAULT OF THROWING.

9. A bird shall be called a "no bird" if thrown broken from the trap, or if, in the opinion of the Referee, it be not fairly thrown; and it shall be counted a "no bird" whether fired at or not.

"NO BIRDS" IF EXTRA ONES ACCIDENTALLY THROWN.

10. In cases where a bird or birds are accidentally released so as to be flying in the air at the same time as the bird or birds at which the shooter is required to fire, it shall be counted a "no bird."

"NO BIRDS" FROM FAULT OF GUN, ETC.

11. If the shooter's gun, being properly loaded and cocked, fails to fire at all from any cause whatever, excepting through the fault of the shooter, the bird shall be counted a "no bird." If the gun misses fire with the first barrel, and the shooter fires the second and "breaks," the shot shall be scored a "kill;" but if he fires the second and misses, it shall be scored a "miss;" and if he does not fire the second it shall be "no bird." If the gun misses fire with the second barrel, the shooter shall be allowed another bird, using a cartridge primed and loaded with powder, but without a charge of shot, in the first barrel, and a loaded cartridge in the second barrel; and he shall pull the trigger of the first barrel after the trap has been released.

KILLS.

12. A bird to be scored a "kill" must have a piece visibly broken from it whilst in the air. The Referee shall be the sole judge as to whether a bird is broken, and any person impugning his decision shall be disqualified from the current competition. No bird shall under any circumstances be retrieved for examination.

CLUB SCORE BOOKS.

13. Every Club affiliated to the Association shall keep an official score book, showing in detail the results of every competition, and

INANIMATE BIRDS. 117

such score book shall always be available for examination by any person duly authorised by the Association. Broken birds or "kills" shall be indicated by the figure one (1), and missed birds by a nought (0).

BETTING AT CLUBS.

14. No betting shall be allowed.

Special Rules for Continuous Fire.

POSITION OF SHOOTERS.

15. There shall be six shooters for the five marks. Five shooters shall occupy the five marks, and No. 6 shooter shall stand behind No. 1 waiting his turn. No. 1 shooter shall fire first from No. 1 mark, No. 2 shooter from No. 2 mark, and so on in rotation down the line. At or during the completion of the round, No. 1 shall take the place of No. 2, and No. 6 shall occupy No. 1 mark, No. 2 shooter shall occupy No. 3 mark, and so on, No. 5 becoming the shooter in waiting behind No. 1.

"NO. 1." "PULL."

16. When the shooter is at the mark, the puller shall call the number, and the shooter shall then call "Pull."

FIRING OUT OF TURN.

17. If a shooter fire out of turn, the bird shall be a "no bird," and the shooter who fired out of turn shall lose his shot, and be judged to have missed.

UNKNOWN ANGLES.

18. When the traps are set to throw at unknown angles, and there are two or more traps behind each screen, the puller should be informed by some suitable means which trap behind each screen he is to pull, so that the shooter shall be kept in ignorance of the angle at which his bird will be thrown.

Special Rules for Single Fire Competitions at Unknown Traps.

POSITION OF SHOOTER.

19. The shooter shall stand at the centre mark and fire at five birds before leaving the line.

"READY." "PULL."

20. When the shooter is at the mark, and prepared to fire, the puller shall call "Ready," and the shooter shall then call "Pull."

118   SHOOTING.

ORDER OF RELEASING FIVE TRAPS.

21. In cases where there is only one trap at each position, all five traps shall be filled before the shooter commences to shoot. The Referee may indicate to the puller, by means of a pack of five cards, each bearing the number of an individual trap (1, 2, 3 , 4, 5), the order in which the traps are to be pulled. The cards shall be the remaining cards, and then turn them up one at a time until five birds have been shot at. In the event of a "no bird," the trap throwing it shall be at once re-filled, and the Referee shall re-shuffle the remaining cards, and then turn them up one at a time until five birds have been shot at.

ORDER OF RELEASING TEN TRAPS.

22. In cases where there are two traps at each position, all ten shall be filled before the shooter commences to shoot. The Referee shall indicate to the puller by means of a pack of ten cards (or other suitable device) the order in which the traps are to be pulled. The cards, which shall bear the number of an individual trap (1A, 1B, 2A, 2B, etc), should be shuffled for each shooter, and turned up one at a time until five birds have been shot at, the next card to be taken when a "no bird" is thrown.

ORDER OF RELEASING FIFTEEN TRAPS.

23. In cases where there are three traps at each position, the same conditions as in the preceding rule shall apply, except that, instead of ten cards, fifteen shall be used, marked 1A, 1B, 1C, 2A, 2B, 2C, etc.

Special Rules for Single-Fire Competitions at Unknown Traps with Double Rises.

POSITION OF SHOOTER.

24. The shooter shall stand at the centre mark and fire at five pairs of birds before leaving the line.

"READY." "PULL."

25. When the shooter is at the mark and prepared to fire, the puller shall call "Ready," and the shooter shall then call "Pull."

SCORING DOUBLE RISES.

26. One point shall be given for each bird killed in a double-rise competition, and a shooter shall be entitled to fire both barrels at one bird.

ORDER OF RELEASING TRAPS.

27. Any suitable means, such as a pack of cards, each numbered or marked to correspond with an individual trap, shall be used. Two

INANIMATE BIRDS. 119

cards shall be drawn simultaneously, and the puller shall release the corresponding traps when the shooter calls " Pull."

Handicapping and Shooting Off Ties.

BY POINTS.

28. Handicapping shall be on the system of giving points, the numbers varying from 2 to 7.

BASED ON PAST SCORES.

29. The handicap points allowed shall be as nearly as possible one point for every 10 per cent. of misses (out of birds shot at) recorded against the shooter during the month on which the handicap is calculated, it being understood that no account shall be taken of fractions of 1 per cent., and also that, should the percentage work out midway between any two values of points, the shooter shall be awarded the larger handicap allowance.

PERIODIC REVISION OF HANDICAPS.

30. Each competitor shall be re-handicapped at the end of each calendar month, provided he shall have fired at not less than 100 birds during that period, and no fresh handicap shall be calculated for him until he shall have fired at 100 birds at least since his last handicap was framed.

PENALTY POINTS.

31. A shooter shall be penalised one point for each and every prize or sweepstakes over the subscribed or declared value of 20s. he may win during the current month ; this penalty, and any additional ones subsequently incurred, to continue in force until a new handicap is calculated. In the event of a division, the shooters dividing must arrange and declare which of them shall be penalised. This system of penalties shall equally apply to the winners of scratch events, but it shall not apply to the winning holdership of trophies, nor to the winner of rounds in the I.B.S.A. medal competitions.

LIMITED VARIATION OF POINTS.

32. The points awarded to a shooter at the beginning of each month shall not be varied by more than one point from the points he possessed, as a result of averages and penalties, at the end of the previous month. This rule shall not apply to new members, whose points shall be allotted at the end of their first month, as laid down in Rule 31, provided in all cases that no such handicap shall be allotted until a new member has fired at not less than 100 birds since joining the club.

120 SHOOTING.

TIES.

33. Ties shall be shot off at not less than ten birds each shooter in handicap events.

LIMIT SCORE.

34. The highest score possible in each ten-bird competition shall be twelve points, and in similar proportion for competitions of a greater number of birds.

PENALTY FOR OPTIONAL SWEEPSTAKES.

35. In the case of an optional sweepstakes being added to a special competition, it shall be treated as a separate event on the question of penalties.

POINTS FOR NEW MEMBERS.

36. Every new member joining a club shall be allowed four handicap points, unless he is already a member of some other affiliated club, in which case his points at that club shall be given him in the new club; in the event of his belonging to more than one other club, and having different points in them, the points allotted to him in the new club shall be the smaller number.

The " Rose " System of Dividing Sweepstakes.

NUMBER OF DIVISIONS.

37. The Club shall decide whether the shooters making the two top scores, or the three top scores (or any other suitable combination), shall participate in the division of the pool.

PROPORTIONS FOR EACH ORDER OF MERIT.

38. Having decided what scores shall entitle the shooters to a share in the pool, the Club shall determine what number of shares shall be allotted to each order of merit, such as three shares for each shooter making the top score, two shares for the second score, and one share for the third score—or six shares, four shares, and one share respectively, as may be decided.

SCRATCH AND HANDICAP EVENTS.

39. This method of dividing pools shall be equally applicable to scratch and handicap events.

METHOD OF CALCULATING SHARES.

40. In dividing the money, the number of shooters making the top score shall be multiplied by the number of shares allotted to those

making such score; in the same way the number of shooters making the second score shall be multiplied by the corresponding shares allotted to each, and the shares for the third score shall be similarly worked out. After deducting for birds used, etc., the amount remaining in the pool shall be divided by the total number of shares. The winners shall then be paid at the rate of three such shares to each of the shooters making the top score, and so on among the other shooters, according to the proportions decided upon by the Club.

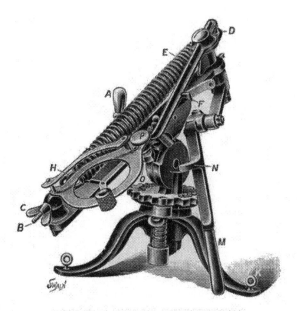

IMPROVED MODEL "SWIFTSURE."

LEGAL SEASONS FOR KILLING GAME, ETC.

Under the head of "Game," strictly so-called, are included, throughout the United Kingdom, grouse, blackgame, pheasants, partridges, and hares; for the practically extinct bustard may be left out of consideration for ordinary purposes, and the ptarmigan is only to be found in Scotland. The season for partridges in Ireland was altered in 1899 to correspond with the season in England. In Ireland, quails and landrails are included among "game"; but, although not so designated in the Game Acts relating to Great Britain, these birds cannot be legally shot without a game licence; and a similar remark may be made with regard to woodcock and snipe, under the Game Licences Act, 23 and 24 Vict., cap. 90. The seasons are as follows:—

Kinds of Game.	ENGLAND AND WALES.		SCOTLAND.		IRELAND.	
	Begins.	Ends.	Begins.	Ends.	Begins.	Ends.
Grouse or Moor Fowl	August 12	Dec. 10	August 12	Dec. 10	August 12	Dec. 10
Blackgame, or Heath Fowl	August 20*	Dec. 10	August 20	Dec. 10	August 20	Dec. 10
Ptarmigan...	...	...	August 12	Dec. 10	...	...
Partridge	Sept. 1	Feb. 1	Sept. 1	Feb. 1	Sept. 1	Feb. 1
Pheasant	October 1	Feb. 1	October 1	Feb. 1	October 1	Feb. 1
Quail	As Wild Birds.		As Wild Birds.		Sept. 20	Jan. 10
Landrail	Ditto	Ditto	Ditto	Ditto	Sept. 20	Jan. 10
Bustard	Sept. 1	March 1	Ditto	Ditto	Sept. 1	Jan. 10
Hare	No Close Season.		No Close Season.†		August 12	April 20
Male Fallow Deer...	Ditto	Ditto	Ditto	Ditto	June 10	Sept. 29
Other Male Deer	Ditto	Ditto	Ditto	Ditto	June 10	Dec. 31
Wildfowl and other Birds not game § ...	August 1	March 1	August 1	March 1	August 1	March 1

* Except in Somerset, Devon, and the New Forest, where the commencement of blackgame shooting is deferred until September 1.

† By the Hares Preservation Act, 1892, the sale of Hares and Leverets in Great Britain is prohibited from March 1 to July 31 inclusive, under Penalty of 20s., unless received from abroad.

§ Upon the recommendation of County Councils, the Home Secretary has made orders to vary the close time in a great many counties too numerous to mention here. Particulars may be obtained in any county from the Clerk of the Peace.—"The Rural Almanac."

FOR HEALTHY BROODS
⸺ USE ⸺

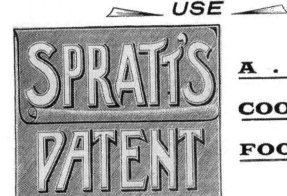

A . . . COOKED . FOOD. . . .

IN 3 GRADES:
COARSE,
MEDIUM,
OR FINE.

TRADE MARK

A TONIC GAME SPICE.

Dust a little over the Food in Cold or Inclement Weather, or when there is any tendency to Diarrhœa.

YOUR TRADESMAN WILL SUPPLY YOU.

Samples of Food post free of

SPRATT'S PATENT LTD.,
24 & 25, Fenchurch Street, London, E.C.

CHAMBERLIN'S
PHEASANTS' FOOD,

 Wild Duck Meal,

PARTRIDGE MEAL,

SPECIAL GROUSE FOOD.

Write for the new Book of Prices, with Treatise on Pheasant Rearing, free by post.

KALŸDE,

A VOLATILE POWDER

The only Cure for Gapes in Pheasants & Poultry.

2/4 per Tin, Post Free.

JAMES CHAMBERLIN & SMITH,

Game, Poultry, & Dog Food Warehouse,

POST OFFICE STREET, NORWICH.

MODERN GUN FACTORY.

EDITOR, *Field*, July 17.—"The work there produced being unsurpassed by anything in the Market."

THE "VICTOR"

Single or Double Trigger.

Extra Quality, only 55 Guineas, Cash.

BADMINTON LIBRARY.—"Stood a deal of rough work and acted very well. Certainly deserves our praise."

With "VICTOR" Certificate of Maintenance for Seven Years.
(Vide Price List and Certificate.)

THIS GUN, London made throughout, cannot be too highly recommended as an embodiment of the highest quality, perfect design, handiness, finish, and specially suitable for a great deal of hard work.

BADMINTON LIBRARY.—"A best London gun is somewhat superior as regards strength and excellence of shooting, but it is immensely superior in finish and general appearance, as well as in its balance."

COGSWELL & HARRISON, Ltd.,
141, NEW BOND STREET; 226, STRAND.

Small Arms Factory—Gillingham Street, near Victoria Station.

LONDON.

KYNOCH SPORTING AMMUNITION.

— Specialities. —

THE "GROUSE."
THE "P. G."
THE "KYNOID" (WATERPROOF).

Loaded with Kynoch Smokeless Powder, Kynoch Cartridges give the maximum of killing effect with the minimum of unpleasantness in the shape of recoil, smoke, fumes, etc.

KYNOCH SMOKELESS POWDER.

KYNOCH LIMITED, BIRMINGHAM (ETC.)

London Office: JAMES ST., HAYMARKET, S.W.

Contractors to the British Government.

The Cogswell & Harrison
SYSTEM OF
Single Trigger Guns.
22 GUINEAS TO 55 GUINEAS CASH.

Editor, FIELD, March 26th:—"The mechanism is of the simplest possible character. We have done our best to make it fail, but have not been able to do so. The one we here notice will be classed among the 'survival of the fittest.'"

THE C. & H. OPTIONAL SINGLE TRIGGER, so as to fire either barrel first, One Guinea extra, Victors excepted.

THE "AVANT TOUT."

The FIELD:—"Simplest self-ejector. After severe test we can thoroughly recommend it."
MANY THOUSANDS IN USE. 15 GUINEAS TO 55 GUINEAS CASH.
HAMMERLESS GUNS FROM 15 GUINEAS CASH.

"GRAND PRIX" PIGEON GUN.
SEASON 1900 TO MARCH 21 ONLY.

MONTE CARLO.—Prix Briasco; Prix d'Ouverture; Prix de Stand; Prix de Janvier; Prix de Blondin.
HENDON.—Grand International Champion Stakes (21 out of 22).
Besides many other first-class prizes.

"*Grand Prix*" Pigeon Guns excel for *Hard Shooting. High Penetration. Regular Patterns.*

N.B.—A "Grand Prix" with Single Trigger recommended.

COGSWELL & HARRISON, LTD.
226, Strand; 141, New Bond Street, London.

ELEY'S WATERPROOF "PEGAMOID" SPORTING CARTRIDGES

Loaded T.S. Black,

Amberite, Riflite, Walsrode, or Cooppal Powder.

Also in Green, Blue,

With Schultze, Cannonite, or Ballistite Powder.

And Various Colours.

ALSO MILITARY & REVOLVER CARTRIDGES
of Every Description, with either Black or Smokeless Powder.

Eley's Expert Trap.

WITH CORDITE.

Eley's Repau Trap.

GR 230

230 LONG

FOR TRAP SHOOTING.

COLT & WEBLEY TARGET.

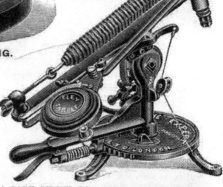

WEBLEY POCKET 32.

FELT & CARD GUN WADS

Nickel Coated Bullets.

Of all Gunmakers & Dealers, wholesale only.

NOTE.—Sportsmen should ask for ELEY'S, and see that the name is on the TUBE or BASE.

WEBLEY, MARK III., 3.

"SWIFTSURE"

Traps and Birds.
(REGISTERED).

Introduced in 1888.
The Leading Trap ever since
Used by
Home and Colonial Clubs.

One Quality only—
"THE BEST."

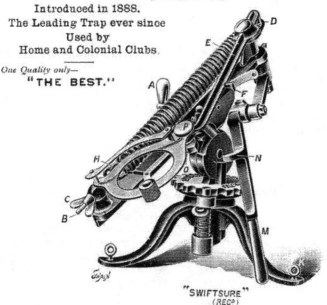

"SWIFTSURE"
(REGD)

TRAPS.
SIMPLICITY OF MECHANISM.

Finest Extant, Single	Cash	**25/-**
Improved Model Ditto	,,	**35/-**
Double Rise Ditto	,,	**52/6**

Accessories for Fixing, &c., extra on Single Rise 5/-,
Double Rise, 7/- cash.

BIRDS.— SWIFTSURES are the Standard Birds for best quality in the Market. Travel well. Fly well. Break well.
Per 500 Barrel, cash 15/-   Per 100 Box, cash, 5/-

OFFICIAL RULES AND SCORE BOOK POST FREE ON APPLICATION.

"Swiftsure" Traps and Birds can be obtained from all Gunmakers and Dealers.

THE "PAYNE-GALLWEY" CARTRIDGE BAG.

Sole Makers— GEO. G. BUSSEY and Co.

GENUINE BAGS ARE BRANDED THUS:

'Payne-Gallwey' ⇐GGB⇐

Avoid Cheap Imitations.

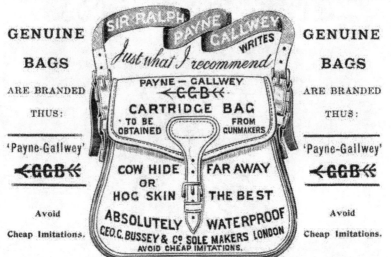

GENUINE BAGS ARE BRANDED THUS:

'Payne-Gallwey' ⇐GGB⇐

Avoid Cheap Imitations.

THOUSANDS ARE GIVING COMPLETE SATISFACTION.

PATENT "EASY CATCH" SLIP

Sole Makers: GEO. G. BUSSEY & Co.

THE MOST PERFECT SLIP INVENTED.

The Slip can be instantly secured to the ring on the dog's collar with very little exertion, by the single motion of *one hand only*. The releasing is still more easily accomplished by pulling the knob at end of cord, thereby drawing the bolt clear of the ring, when the dog is immediately set free. No jerk or sharp pulling is required, and the action can be performed without any variation in the attitude of the operator. Its construction is exceedingly simple, and has none of its mechanism exposed.

The *Field* says:—"Appears to be an excellent contrivance."

GEO. G. BUSSEY & Co.'s SHOOTING REQUISITES
Are to be obtained from high-class Gun Makers.

"CERTUS" RIFLES.

Self-Ejector.   Efficient Safety.   Detachable Barrel.

Accuracy of Shooting unsurpassed.
THE SIGHTING OF EVERY RIFLE CAREFULLY ADJUSTED.

"Certus" back sights, interchangeable.   "Certus" foresight.

"CERTUS" RIFLES.

Bore.			Cash.
·220 {	**Expert Marksman's,** plain finish ...	£2	2	0
	Ditto. engraved, and better finish	3	3	0
·295)	**Rook and Rabbit Rifle,** plain finish ...	3	3	0
or }	Ditto. engraved, and better finish	5	5	0
·250)	Ditto. best quality, handsome stock	8	8	0

CARTRIDGES.

·220	"Certus" ...	...	...	...	per 100	1/2 cash.
	Ditto.	long range	...	...	,,	1/8 cash.
·295	Ditto.	...	...	...	...	,,	4/6 cash.
·256	Ditto.	...	...	...	...	,,	3/9 cash.

COGSWELL & HARRISON, Ltd.,
226, STRAND; 141, NEW BOND STREET, LONDON.

BELL & PRICHARD,

2, LUDGATE CIRCUS,

London, E.C.,

OPPOSITE COOK'S TOURIST OFFICES.

➤ SHOOTING ➤

AND

FISHING OUTFITS,

A SPECIALTY.

Shooting Suits from 50s.   All Goods Thoroughly Shrunk

NORFOLK SUITS from 45s.

BREECHES AND GAITERS

From 42s.

SCOTCH TWEED KNICKERS

From 12s. 6d.

TESTED CARTRIDGES,

WITH

SELECTED SMOKELESS POWDER.

An unbroken successful Record of 20 Years!
THE VICTOR, Standard for Price and Quality, 1900.

N.B.—The constantly increasing price of Loading Materials has been met by us by a constantly increasing output—so much so that our Selling Prices are this season reduced, whilst quality is maintained.

Embodiment of finest materials

Paper Cases 9/- cash per 100
Waterproof Cases 10/- ,,
Brass-covered ,, 10/6 ,,

Unsurpassed for efficiency of shooting.

8/- cash per 100.

Reduced length Cartridge, with 1oz. shot.

8/- cash per 100.

Reliability and economy.

7/6 cash per 100
6/6 ,, with black powder.

CARRIAGE FREE for Orders of 1,000 sent in one Consignment to any Station in Great Britain by Goods Trains.
CARRIAGE PAID for consignments of less than 1,000 to Scotch Stations—Cash, 3s. 3d. To English or Welsh Stations—Cash—2s. 6d. Cartridges by Passenger Train are generally charged the usual Parcel Rates.
CARRIAGE ALLOWANCE of 4s. on Orders of 1,000 to Ireland, Purchaser paying Carriage.
ALL WOOD PACKING CASES FREE. CHILLED SHOT, 3D. PER 100 EXTRA NET.

COGSWELL & HARRISON, Ltd.,
London: 141, New Bond Street; 226, Strand.

AN IDEAL PAPER FOR SPORTSMEN:

THE

SHOOTING TIMES

Bright, Instructive, Readable. Deals thoroughly with three subjects :—

Shooting. Fishing. Dogs.

EXPERTS IN ALL DEPARTMENTS.

PRICE - - 10/10 per Year, or 2d. Weekly.

IF YOU WANT A GUN!
IF YOU WANT A SHOOT!
IF YOU WANT A DOG!
IF YOU WANT A KEEPER!
IF YOU WANT ANYTHING!

In the Sporting World,

Advertise in the Miscellaneous columns of

The Shooting Times

If you have a dog or gun or anything for sale, you will not find a cheaper or better medium.

SMALL "WANTED" ADVERTISEMENTS

20 WORDS - - - 1s.

OFFICES: 72 TO 76 TEMPLE CHAMBERS, BOUVERIE STREET
FLEET STREET, E.C.

THE BEST TRULY SMOKELESS

Sporting Powder.

"E.C."  No. 3.

NO SMOKE.   NO BLOWBACK.

QUICK IGNITION.   REDUCED HEATING AND RECOIL.

TRADE   MARK.

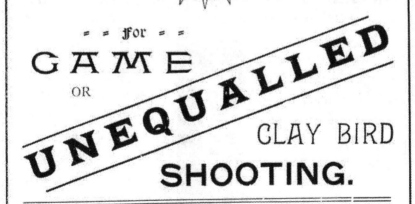

= = For = =
GAME
OR
CLAY BIRD SHOOTING.

UNEQUALLED

The E.C. Powder Company, Ltd.,
40, NEW BROAD STREET, LONDON, E.C.

'Blagdon' Shooting School

(Frequent trains to Malden or Raynes Park Station, ¼ mile; also Wimbledon Station, 2 miles).

GUN FITTING by SPECIALISTS

At BLAGDON (open-air range); or in LONDON (enclosed range).

The Most Hon. the MARQUIS OF GRANBY:—" . . Thoroughly practical and convenient."

TO SHOOT WELL, USE A GOOD-FITTING GUN.

"BLAGDON" OPEN-AIR RANGE;

"LONDON" ENCLOSED RANGE.

THE GUN STOCK OF EVERY SPORTSMAN SHOULD FIT TO A NICETY SHOULD HE WISH TO SHOOT HIS BEST.

Editor FIELD:—"*An exceedingly ingenious principle. Handy Trygun, much lighter than usual.*"

Shooting Lessons by Expert Instructors

COUNTY GENTLEMAN:—"*The best of such Schools.*"

At Blagdon the services of an experienced Coach are always obtainable to give advice to those sportsmen who require tuition in the art of Shooting.

A series of visits will enable the young shooter, or one who has commenced later in life, to have confidence in the field, and necessarily a greater average of kills to his credit.

UNLIMITED PRACTICE.
Season's Subscription Tickets now issued, 2 Guineas net.